FISHING THE REEFS

BY PETER DUNN-RANKIN

MUTUAL PUBLISHING

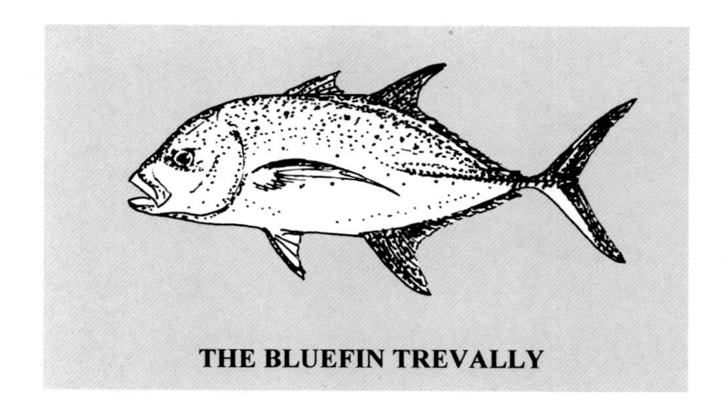
THE BLUEFIN TREVALLY

CONTENTS

Spinning into the white water of Ngatangiia Passage on Rarotonga's east coast.

INTRODUCTION

It has been my fortune to spin a surface lure along the edges of some of the finest reefs in the world. These have included the virgin sunken reefs off Naigani Island in Fiji, the bracelet shoals of mysterious Yap, the barrier reefs of Belau, the borders of untouched Fanning Island in Kiribati and the fringing reefs off Kaho'olawe in Hawai'i.

These and other great fishing spots have yielded such monstrous hits that they are almost beyond description. I can remember whipping green and white topwater lures across the coral humps southwest of Cook Island in Kiribati. There I watched giant trevally, their backs breaking the surface in a path eight inches wide, engulf such offerings and take them to never-never land. I gave up lure after lure just to see such action.

On the island of Yap, where native islanders still use stone money, I was viewed with wonder. An old chief fingered my 12-lb. test monofilament line, looked at the 35-lb. trevally (jack) that I had put on the dock and muttered under his breath. I remember that I once caught four fish in four casts while drifting over the brightly colored inside reef. The fish (snapper, grouper, wrasse, and blue jack) were as brightly colored as their surroundings. On my fifth cast a red-eyed snapper in the 15-lb. range took the small round-headed Dillinger home under a rock, and that was the end of that lure. Stories of that day were circulated, and people say that the natives still remember the fisherman who was magic.

But there is no mystery. Modern technology and knowledge of the Pacific islands can make us all magicians. Over the years I invented and perfected the resin popper with a urethane core. The **PILI** lure is still sold in Hawaii by a Kona company and is found in major fishing catalogs. My more recent lures, the **MULI** and the super **LOLO,** have accounted for many all-tackle and line-class world records. In a later chapter I illustrate how you, also, can make the world's best fishing lure.

The edge of the Pacific coral reef is a last great frontier for the sport fisherman. The isolated reefs of the Pacific are one of the few places where fish over 100 lbs. will still fearlessly attack cast surface plugs. Surprisingly, spinning on or near the edge of the reef is an innovation in most parts of the Pacific. Pacific islanders, for example, troll away from the white water, where all the action is. That is why, even on well-populated atolls, the topwater reef angler can make his mark.

Fishing the Reefs prepares you to enjoy the thrill of fishing different Pacific islands. This book will tell you **Where to Go, What to Take** and **How to Fish.** While this text concentrates on the Pacific coral reef, its techniques apply to reefs in the Caribbean Sea, Indian Ocean and elsewhere.

Over the years I have learned to be a better fisherman and to enjoy it more. Now I lose fewer lures and catch more fish and bigger fish. This book is a product of a lifetime of fishing experiences. But there has been a great deal of experimentation and study, as well. ***Fishing the Reefs*** illustrates successful ways to topwater-fish the myriad reefs of the South Pacific. The text also includes a few adventures in the islands and provides a glimpse of the possibilities for any adventurous angler.

Dick Gushman catches a papio (small jack) on a PILI lure, spinning in the lagoon in back of English Harbor, Fanning Island, Kiribati.

WHERE TO GO

When one spreads out a map of the Pacific and looks at the islands and coral reefs dotting the sea frontier, it is easy to understand that the main problem is "getting there,". While a few small reef islands are so isolated that they can be reached only by a long inter-island boat trip, many are just a short plane-hop away from the jet airports at the centers of the main Pacific islands. Now there is great topwater reef fishing within the reach of any enterprising fisherman.

How to Get There

There are two major airline hubs in the Pacific. They are **Honolulu**, Hawai'i and **Nadi**, Fiji. You can fly to these hubs from San Francisco or Los Angeles or from Sydney or Auckland, perhaps touching a few islands in between (See Pacific Airline Routes, p. 4). The major carriers are **Air New Zealand, Polynesian Airlines, Continental Airlines, Air France, Qantas and Air Nauru.**

From Hawai'i you can fly to all the major island centers, as well as Tonga, Samoa, Tahiti, Micronesia, Guam, the Marianas, Rarotonga, Nauru and Kiribati. From Nadi you can get to Vanuatu, New Caledonia, Tuvalu, Wallis and Futuna, Tonga, the Solomons, Kiribati, Nauru and Rarotonga. Major carriers like Air France also go on to the Cook Islands, Fiji and New Caledonia.

On each of the main islands there are usually local airlines that "spoke-out" to other

Air Distances from Hawai'i to the Pacific Islands

Nation (Island/City)	Miles	Hours
Cook Islands (Rarotonga)	2950	7
Federated Micronesia (Pohnpei)	3090	9
Fiji (Nadi)	3160	7
French Polynesia (Tahiti)	2740	6
Guam (Agana)	3800	8
Hawai'i (Honolulu)	——	-
Kiribati (Christmas)	1200	3
Marshall Is. (Majuro)	2270	6
Nauru (Yaren)	3700	9
New Caledonia (Noumea)	4000	9
Northern Marianas (Saipan)	3704	9
Papua New Guinea (Port Moresby)	5000	11
Solomon Is. (Honiara)	4450	11
Tokelau Is. (Nukunonu)	3500	8
Tonga (Nuku'alofa)	3200	8
Tuvalu (Funifuti)	3800	9
Vanuatu (Port Vila)	3750	9
Wallis & Futuna (Uvea)	3550	9
Western Samoa (Apia)	2500	6

When flying from the west coast of the U.S., add 2500 miles and five hours for a stopover in Hawai'i

Airline prices vary between $600 to $1800 US. From Hawai'i the average round trip fare is around $900 US.

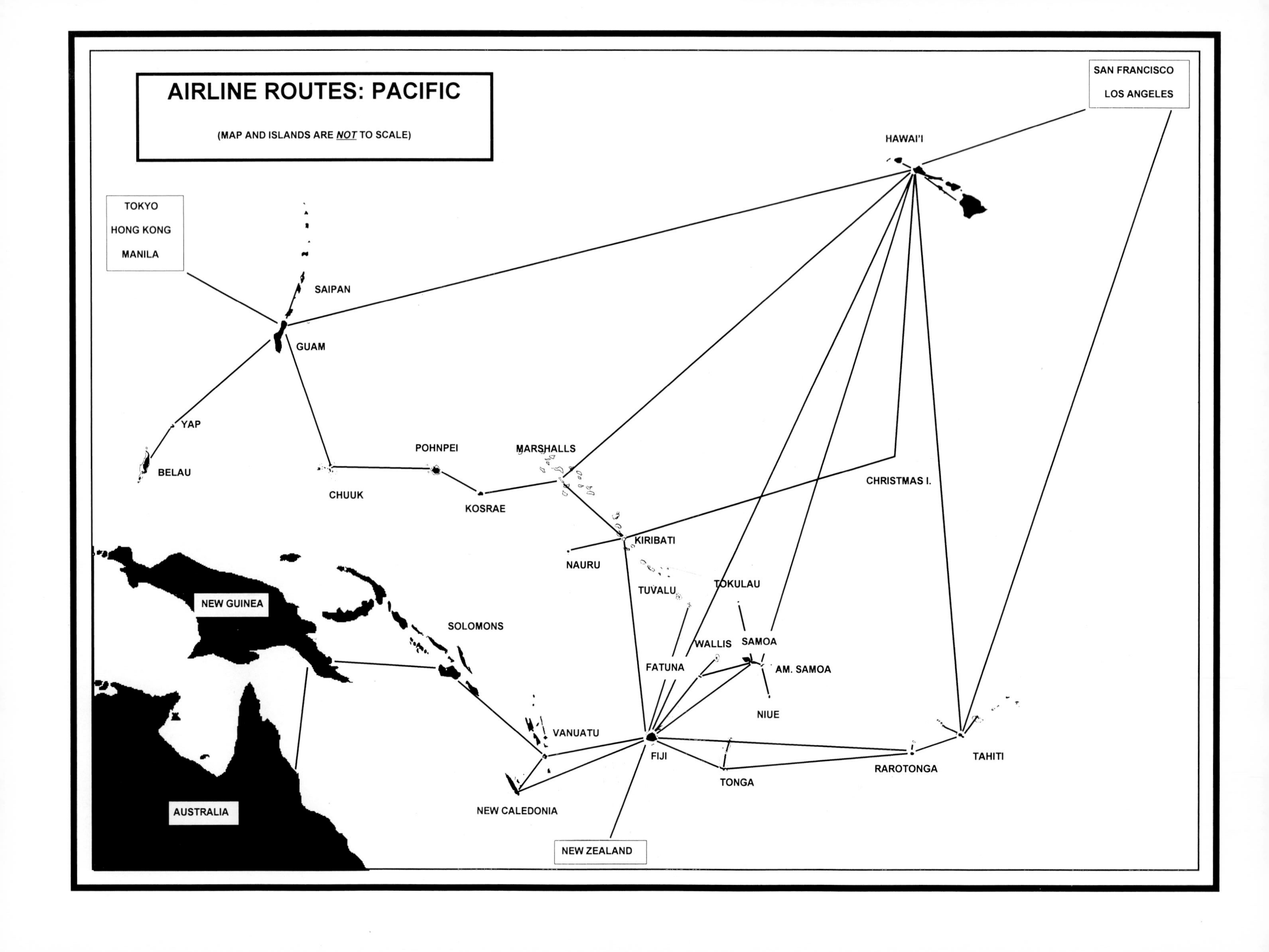
AIRLINE ROUTES: PACIFIC
(MAP AND ISLANDS ARE NOT TO SCALE)
SAN FRANCISCO
LOS ANGELES
HAWAI'I
TOKYO
HONG KONG
MANILA
SAIPAN
GUAM
YAP
BELAU
CHUUK
POHNPEI
KOSRAE
MARSHALLS
CHRISTMAS I.
KIRIBATI
NAURU
TUVALU
TOKULAU
NEW GUINEA
SOLOMONS
WALLIS
SAMOA
FATUNA
AM. SAMOA
NIUE
VANUATU
FIJI
TAHITI
RAROTONGA
TONGA
AUSTRALIA
NEW CALEDONIA
NEW ZEALAND

inhabitable islands in the area. From Nuku'alofa in Tonga you can fly **Royal Tongan Airlines** to its outer islands such as Ha'apai or Vava'u. From Papeete, Tahiti, you can fly a local airline to the leeward islands or Rangiroa on **Air Tahiti**. Then there is **Air Vanuatu, Air Rarotonga, Samoa Air, Air Caledonie, Air Marshall Islands, Solomon Airlines, Air Niugini, Fiji Air** and **Sun Flower Airlines,** also in Fiji. For more detailed information, Frommer's latest *Comprehensive Travel Guide to the South Pacific* is the best reference. Another good source of information is *Micronesia: A Travel Survival Kit* by Bendure and Friary.

Air, ground or boat travel to good fishing spots that are away from the capitals or major centers of commerce adds to the initial travel costs, but is usually worth the expense. Good fishing and great adventure in the Cooks, for example, is found by taking a local flight from Rarotonga to an outer island such as Aitutaki. The round-trip cost may be an additional 10 percent. Good fishing in Fiji is found away from the main island of Viti Levu and a small additional cost will be involved. If you want to fish Yap, in the Federated States of Micronesia, you first fly to Guam, then for a nominal additional amount, take a short flight south, and stop on the way to Belau.

While the distances in the Pacific are vast, modern jet travel has made all the major island states or nations relatively accessible. The accompanying table lists the approximate distance and flying time from Hawai'i to the countries, states or territories that comprise the Pacific Islands.

Deighton Emmons spins the big break near the village of Tafua in Eastern Savai'i, Western Samoa

Fishing Potential of the Pacific

Air travel is a major concern in fishing the reefs of the Pacific. Travel time and costs, however, do not provide a complete picture of the possibilities in the Pacific. Of prime importance to most adventurers is "How good is the fishing?" and "Will I see and experience something new?" The accompanying table judges the fishing and adventure potential of the South Pacific islands.

I have rated twenty-two island states or nations on a scale of 22 (the best) to 1 (the worst) on each of the following characteristics: fishing potential (**Fish**), housing and meals (**House**), accessibility (**Access**), adventure (**Advent**), low population density (**Pop**) and shortest travel time (**Time**). Population density is based on the population of each area divided by its linear miles of reef. Travel time is based on departure from Honolulu, Hawai'i.

The table to the right provides these rank **values** and the fishing areas have been given an overall score in the **Total** column based on these ratings. The **higher** the score, the **better** the overall rating. The scale provides a picture of the most promising areas in which to go fishing.

Leading the way are **Fiji**, **Belau** (Palau), the **Federated States**

Ranking the New Pacific Islands in Six Areas Related to Fishing

Island	Fish	House	Access	Advent	Pop	Time	Total
American Samoa	1	13	16	3	4	20	57
Belau	20	19	14	19	17	7	96
Cook Islands	10	17	15	16	11	15	84
Federated Micronesia	19	11	18	20	16	13	97
Fiji	22	14	19	14	18	19	99
French Polynesia	15	18	20	8	14	17	92
Guam	2	18	21	1	3	12	57
Hawai'i	5	21	20	9	7	22	84
Kiribati	21	10	10	13	15	21	90
Marshall Islands	14	8	17	7	12	20	78
Nauru	3	9	6	4	1	4	27
New Caledonia	17	12	8	15	20	8	80
Niue	12	3	7	5	9	11	47
Northern Marianas	6	20	12	2	10	10	60
Papua New Guinea	14	9	3	22	22	3	73
Solomon Islands	18	4	2	21	21	6	72
Tokelau	9	6	1	11	6	1	34
Tonga	11	15	11	17	8	14	76
Tuvalu	7	1	4	12	2	2	26
Vanuatu	16	16	9	18	19	9	87
Wallis & Futuna	13	2	5	10	13	5	48
Western Samoa	4	7	13	6	15	16	61

When using this table "look out" for low numbers in areas that are important to you. A low number means potential difficulty.

of Micronesia, and **French Polynesia**. While Tahiti, the center of French Polynesia, is reasonably accessible, one needs to go to its outer islands like **Rangiora** to get real topwater action. Fiji is similar to French Polynesia in that the main island of **Viti Levu** is well-populated. Great fishing occurs on the outer islands and reefs. As for **Belau,** the only real drawback is the lengthy travel time. Coming from Hawai'i, you first fly to Guam and then down to the main island of **Babledaob** and then by van to **Oreor** (formerly Koror). Once you arrive in Oreor, great fishing is at your doorstep.

The **Federated States of Micronesia** contain the Islands of **Pohnpei** (Ponape), **Kosrae** (Kusaie), **Yap** and **Chuuk** (Truk). Each of these island centers is extremely interesting to visit and each has good fishing off its fringing or barrier reefs. The Japanese occupation of these islands was extensive and remnants of World War II are everywhere. Exploration of the islands is rewarding and an added incentive to go there. Kosrae is the smallest of these states and its accommodations are sparse. It is, however, relatively close to Hawai'i and you can still catch a big 'omilu off its clean reefs.

While each island of Micronesia is fairly accessible, the main islands of Pohnpei, Yap and **Moen** in Chuuk are not physically as large as other highly rated places, and overfishing has occurred close to the population centers.

Hawai'i scores relatively high, primarily based on its accommodations, safety, and proximity. The fishing potential of O'ahu, which is highly populated, is less than average.

Not surprisingly, if you relate the population density to the adventure and topwater fishing potential of the islands, it turns out that the areas with the smallest number of people per linear mile of reef are also some of the best places to go fishing. It is possible, however, to find super fishing in isolated areas or reefs on some of the more densely populated islands. The reefs off **Ni'ihau** in Hawai'i, the **Vava'u** group in Tonga, **Rose Island** in Western Samoa, the islands outside **Tarawa** in Kiribati and the outer atolls of the Marshall Islands are examples, but you may need a boat to get to these places.

Niue, a small, high island south of American Samoa, has a small population but is somewhat difficult to reach. First you must fly to Western Samoa and then hope to catch a flight south. Niue's accommodations are rural but the fishing on Niue could be spectacular. The island's cliffs, however, make shore fishing difficult, so Niue gets downgraded.

While I have never been to **Nauru**, its population density (8,000 people in 21 square kilometers) makes it the most densely populated in the Pacific. **Guam** suffers similar overcrowding, and its reef fishing is not very productive.

It would be interesting to visit the **Tokelaus**, **Wallis and Futuna**, and **Tuvalu.** These small islands are quite isolated and probably have never been hit with the modern technology incorporated in resin-core lures and IM6 graphite-boron rods. If regular air travel to these isolated spots were feasible, their ratings could be upgraded. Sometimes local airlines out of **Apia**, Western Samoa, or **Nadi**, Fiji, fly to these atolls. Of these islands, the Tokelaus appear to have the greatest potential. French is the main language in Wallis and Futuna.

Western and American Samoa are delightful to visit as cultural and scenic adventures, but fishing the main islands leaves much to be desired. In both of the Samoas, conservation has not been practiced on the reefs and the fishing reflects this general lack of concern.

Vanuatu, the **Solomons**, **New Caledonia,** and **Papua New Guinea** in the Western Pacific show the greatest promise as areas for topwater spinning.

Rating the Islands

100 = Great 0 = Poor Risk

Island	Rating
Fiji	100
Belau	98
Federated Micronesia	97
French Polynesia	90
Kiribati	87
Vanuatu	83
Cook Islands	79
Hawaiian Islands	79
Marshall Islands	78
New Caledonia	74
New Guinea	62
Tonga	68
Solomons	63
Western Samoa	48
Northern Marianas	47
Guam	42
American Samoa	41
Wallis and Futuna	30
Niue	25
Tokelau	18
Tuvalu	1
Nauru	0

A quick look at the most promising areas to go fishing. Leading the way is Fiji.

Once again, especially in New Caledonia and Papua New Guinea, one must get outside the main cities. Each of these four countries is in a relative state of flux, politically, and their great fishing potential gets downgraded for safety reasons. **Vanuatu**, however, is a reasonable hop from Nadi, Fiji, and has good accommodations. Its political climate is also the most stable.

Kiribati, the **Marshalls,** and **Tonga** in the Eastern Pacific have a myriad of far-flung atolls that promise the finest fishing in the world. **Christmas** and **Fanning** Islands, among the line islands of Kiribati, are the closest to Hawai'i but regular air service has not been permanently established. At this writing Air Nauru flies to Christmas. These areas offer outstanding fishing for the spincaster, but getting there is the big problem. I am told there is some air service from **Tarawa** to its outer atolls, but you would probably need to spend over a week to make connections. Some of the outer islands of the Marshalls have air service but accommodations are not available. Boat service is sporadic and time-consuming. If you have the time, however, super fishing is possible.

Tonga's leeward reefs close to the main islands are overfished, but the less-accessible eastern or windward reefs and the far western reefs abound with trevally.

Hawai'i has the finest accommodations and you can still catch fish in the Hawaiian Islands. The action, however, is away from urban O'ahu. The islands of Kaho'olawe, Molokai, and Hawai'i are the most productive.

Forewarned is forearmed and studying an area before going should make your chances of success that much greater. I have learned, for example, that the months that begin with "A" (April and August) are the best times to fish in Western Samoa. That is the time when the bluefin trevally is on the prowl in **Falelupo**. And keep in mind that fishing spots well below the equator, such as **Rarotonga**, **Tonga**, and **New Caledonia**, have a season that is in reverse from the Northern Hemisphere. Visit these places in October and November. On the other hand, some risk is involved in any good adventure. Some of the greatest fishing occurs when you go "out of the way."

Other Places for Adventure

There are still plenty of places to go fishing in the Pacific that are virtually unexplored. These sites offer the opportunity for any sports fisherman to be a true pioneer.

Papua New Guinea: Photographer Chris Watanabe tells me that there is a home boat that runs a ten-day trip in and around the **Sepik River.** The ship runs at night, and during the day explorations and fishing trips are taken on the river and to villages along it.

The Solomons: All those places where great battles of World War II took place, **Rabaul, Bougainville, Guadalcanal,** and the **Admiralty Islands,** would be interesting to visit and offer the promise of great topwater spinning. Marine biologist David Itano tells me that the western Solomon islands, away from the capital, **Honiara**, are beautiful, untouched vistas for the sports fisherman.

Southern Japanese Islands: I have recently seen where world-record bluefin trevally have been caught in the **Ogasawara Archipelago** north of Guam. This area and southern **Okinawa** offer the promise of world records.

The Marquesas: These out-of-the-way islands in French Polynesia could be productive if you can get there. They may be reached by copra steamer.

West Coast of Panama and Costa Rica: More big blue runners, roosterfish, trevallys, and other game fish have been caught off the west coast of these Central American countries than almost any other place in the world. An exploration is warranted.

Yellowfin tuna underneath a school of sardines cause the water to erupt like a curtain of fire near the western reef of Belau.

TYPES OF REEFS AND ISLANDS

Almost all topwater spincasting takes place within 100 yds. of a coral reef. Whether you wade inside or take a boat outside, it is useful to recognize the different types of reefs. Fortunately for the fisherman, coral reefs of the world grow where the water is warm. All the New Pacific Islands, most of which owe their very existence to the coral reef, lie in a belt approximately 20 to 25 degrees north and south of the equator, that is within the *Tropics of Cancer* and *Capricorn.* There are very few exceptions. **Kure** ("curry"), the last atoll in the Northwest Hawaiian Island chain, famous **Midway Island,** and a few other reefs lie outside 25 degrees north latitude.

Reef Formation

Reefs vary because of their age. **Fringing reefs** touch and encircle high islands. Examples of islands of this type include all the main islands of Hawai'i, Rarotonga in the Cooks, and Savai'i in Samoa. In these young islands, the fringing reefs are separated from land only by shallow water at high tide.

Barrier reefs, on the other hand, are separated from land by lagoons and channels. Examples of barrier islands include Pohnpei in Federated Micronesia, Aitutaki in the Cooks, and Belau.

Atolls are usually somewhat circular shoals of coral and sand surrounding a lagoon. Examples of atolls include the Marshall Islands, Rangiaroa in French Polynesia, and Christmas Island in Kiribati.

Each of these three types of reef is in a different phase of its evolution. We owe this insight to Charles Darwin, who guessed during his voyage in the *Beagle* (1831 to 1836) that reefs fringing the shore were younger than barrier reefs. He also noted that atolls, the low bracelet islands of the Pacific, were originally formed around high volcanic islands that had long since disappeared.

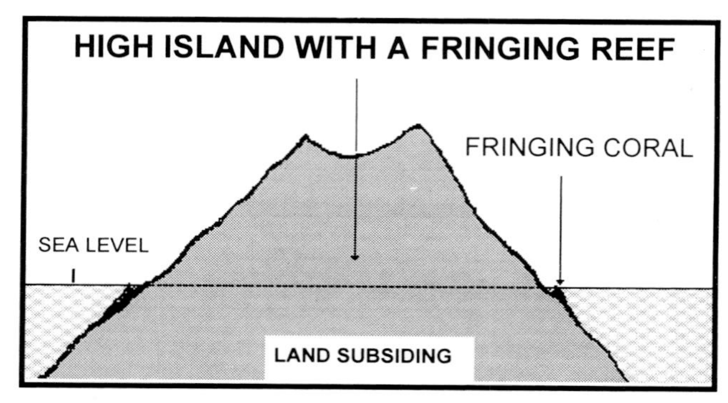

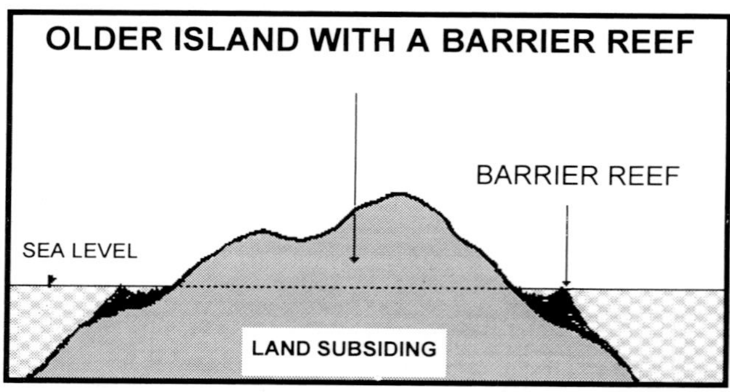

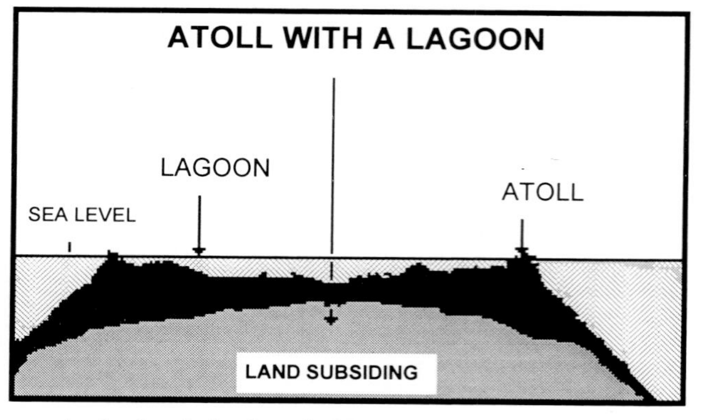

As the land slowly subsides, the coral grows in the waves and sunlight. Because the water in the lagoon is quiet, it may not carry enough oxygen to support the growth of coral.

Coral

There are over 340 species of hard corals. Corals need sunlight and oxygen to survive, and the break of the sea on the shallow reefs is a major source of oxygen. Inside, near the wave break, corals grow low and are densely packed in order to avoid being broken by the crashing surf. There, coralline algae binds the corals together. In the lagoon, however, the water is quiet and most corals do not flourish. The corals that do grow, like staghorn coral, are fragile and easily broken.

Most fringing and barrier reefs have channels or breaks in them (avas), which allow boats and canoes to pass through the coral barrier. These cuts are most often caused by freshwater runoffs from the mountains, or former mountains, to the valley rivers and from there to the sea through the reef. The seaward edges of these channels are often the very best places to catch big fish.

When looking for reefs to fish, check to see that a variety of coral types and colors are available. Many reefs, especially near populated areas, are dead and lifeless. This can be due to freshwater runoff, sewage pollution, the use of chlorine or dynamite to kill fish, or an infestation of the crown-of-thorns starfish. Barren or moribund reefs will generally be unproductive. A check near the surfbreak should reveal a host of small reef fish scuttling in the shallow backwash of each wave. In the slick surface of a forming wave, bright coral and brilliant fish should be visible. If the reef is submerged and you are in a boat, then a quick look over the side with a face mask will reveal the condition of the coral.

Fishing the Different Reefs

The major types of reefs are fished in different ways. The young islands of Hawai'i and Savai'i, for example, have narrow fringing reefs of coral attached to the base of high, black basaltic rocks, which are the result of, geologically speaking, relatively recent lava flows.

Manini (convict tang) on the reef at Hanauma Bay, O'ahu, Hawai'i.

While these reefs are accessible, high surf often makes them difficult to fish, especially for the wading sportsman. In such cases, casts have to be made from high rocks. At higher elevations, the angle that the line makes with the surface of the water will diminish the action of the typical surface lure. Lures that "dig in," like the large Rebel Windcheater, or diving lures, may have to be employed, or the lures may have to be weighted.

Such close fringing reefs are more effectively fished from a boat, with casts made from the seaward side into the reef's edge. There is also less chance of losing fish when spinning from a boat. The hooked gamester can be maneuvered to deeper water without the line becoming cut or frayed on the coral edges of the reef.

Older barrier reefs and atolls, on the other hand, usually have broad areas of reef behind the surfline that offer protection to the wading fisherman. The inside reef is, however, much more susceptible to the tide. Few predators forage inside the reef on an outgoing tide, for example.

Sand flats, usually found between the main island and a barrier reef, are less productive than the edges of a reef. One exception is Christmas Island, the largest atoll in the world. There the giant lagoon is so large it supports the growth of shellfish, milkfish, bonefish and a variety of trevally.

Grass flats can be most effective for the fisherman because the grass supports the growth of young fish and they, in turn, provide food for the larger predators. Within the lagoons of Yap, south of Guam, big fish can be fought with little danger of cutting the line because there are very few coral heads in the grass flats.

In some cases, such as in Fiji, many of the reefs are covered with water. A boat is needed to get to such coral outcroppings. Palau, like Fiji, has a vast lagoon. Its barrier reef stops the Pacific swells, and fishing inside by casting to the break is almost always a pleasure because the surface of the water is usually calm. In addition, there is always a lee shore so it is possible to go outside the reef and fish from the deep water to the reef. It is easier to land larger fish from the deep side.

The best fishing is found near the surfline and close to the channels because the predators patrol the corridor fronting the reef. These bigger fish wait for the rising tide before venturing onto the reef's edge in search of prey. As the surf surges in and out, the reef's reservoir of food is made available.

Sometimes casts must be made from the high rocks.
The edge of the Ka'u Desert on the Big Island of Hawai'i is an example.

Ron Lum lifts a 25 lb. ulua caught off the north coast of Fanning Island, one of the line islands of Kiribati.

Pelagic (open ocean) fish can also be found within 100 yds. of the reef's edge. I have actually caught rainbow runners and tunas while casting into the deep cobalt water just beyond the reef.

Fishing the reefs of the Pacific is very compatible with the sport of scuba diving, because beautiful reefs and clear water are important to both forms of recreation. Dive boats make good platforms for spin fishing and, if an area supports scuba diving, it will generally be productive for the fisherman.

Sometimes a bonanza occurs when tunas attack bait fish inside or close to the reef. Fishermen in small boats and using long poles can spin lures in the midst of this melee and get some great action.

The author sits in a wave on the northwest beach on Anguar, Belau. A blue jack hit a blue-black lure.

Gerald Kobashigawa is "Hooked up" off Ovalau Reef, Fiji

WHAT TO TAKE

What to take with you depends on where you go and how long you plan to stay. For day trips to the islands of Hawai'i, a couple of rods and reels, a dozen good lures and some good hiking boots or shoes will almost suffice. Bringing a backpack that holds some extras (leaders, swivels, etc.) is helpful if you plan to hike. A cooler with ice and a few drinks and a change of clothes that you leave in the rental car will allow you to travel light.

For longer trips, more preparation is needed. In the South Pacific, "7-Elevens" are not found around every corner. If a small plane is part of your travel plans (this is generally true of most fishing expeditions), then weight may be important and you'll need to take less than you normally would. Weight, however, is generally not a consideration when traveling by big jet to destinations like Belau, Pohnpei or Fiji.

It is always good to travel with a fishing partner or two on these adventures. Single items (like a reel-wrench, cooler, fillet knife, gaff, clock, umbrella, etc.) can be "spread around" so that no one person is loaded down and so duplications don't occur. Two, three or four people make a good party. More than four makes it difficult for the group to fit into one vehicle, harder to get reservations, and tougher to keep track of everyone.

A Specific Checklist

Everytime I go fishing I pull out my specific checklist and check off the the items I want to carry on a particular trip. Then I check the items again as I pack each one. Items marked with an asterisk (*) on the list are essential for spinning the reefs of the Pacific islands.

A small plane may restrict how much you can take to an outer island. Here, Cook Island Air lands in Aitutaki.

A Checklist for Traveling and Fishing the Pacific Islands

Paper
*____Tickets
*____Money (If you forget something maybe you can buy it.)
*____Passport (Nice to have. It saves time and hassles.)
____IGFA certificates (Pen, tape, and certified scale are needed for records.)
____Writing paper (Pens)
____Maps (Obtain at map store or local library.)
____Compass (Small, plastic. Helps you relate to chart.)
____Reading materials (For the plane or if the weather turns nasty.)

Fishing Gear
*____Rods ___Light ___Medium ___Heavy. (A long light rod is often best.)
*____Reels ___Light ___Medium ___Heavy. (Include a fast retrieve.)
*____Lines ___Light ___Medium ___Heavy. (IGFA classes include 6- 8-10-12-16-20- and 30-lb test.)
*____Leader (80- or 100-lb. test. J® line, Sevalon® or Sevenstrand® plus sleeves for barracuda.)
*____Lures (MULI, PILI®, LOLO, P. Poppers, Rebel®, Rapala®, Kastmaster®, bucktails & touts.)
*____Hooks ___#2___#3___#4___#5, (Mustad double strength trebles, precut.)
*____Swivels (Straight, barrel and snap)
*____English electricians pliers (For cutting hook eyes, also vise-grip or crimpers, or both)
*____Nail clippers (Sturdy, for cutting leaders.)
____Gaff or Net (There are few good gaffs and no nets on site.)
____Leads (If you bottom fish or want to troll deeper.)
____Gimbals belts (If you go for the big ones.)
____Light harness (For standup trolling between islands.)
____Cotton work gloves (For handling the fish's tail.)
____Fish holding line (To put in a fannypack.)

Clothing
*____Undershorts, shorts or swim trunks, and T-shirts with collar, standard. (Nylon/cotton blend)
*____Jogging shoes, two pairs with heavy socks, or tabis for wading the reef.
*____Hats (Look out for the sun.)
*____Long pants and long-sleeved cotton shirt (Keeps sun off after a burn.)
*____Sunglasses, Polaroid® (Very useful.)
____Tie for Glasses (If surf is high.)
____Long-sleeved flannel shirt (It can be cool at night and after a rain.)
____Light rain gear (Sometimes it pours. A plastic golf jacket is good.)

Checklist Continued

Sundries

*____Sunscreen (15+ SPF, may not be available locally.)
____Toilet articles (Toothpaste and brush, etc.)
____Insect repellent (Sometimes you encounter mosquitos.)
____Dishwashing detergent (Dishes, clothes and showers in hard water.)
____Medical supplies (Include Lomotil®, bandaids, peroxide, Bacitracin®, etc.)
____Seasickness prevention (Transderm V®, Bonine®, rice cakes.)
____Toilet paper (Sometimes not available.)
____Hard candy or snacks (Sometimes a blessing.)
____Tea, coffee or chocolate (To be mixed with hot water.)
____Antiseptic soap (For washing scrapes or cuts.)
____Mosquito net (Helps you sleep at night.)

Miscellaneous

*____Waterproof flashlight (A florescent battery lamp is nice.)
*____Clothes pins (Close to essential for drying shoes and shorts.)
____Alarm clock (If you want to get out early.)
____Camera and film (Your choice but the sun is bright.)
____Mask and fins (Good for a quick check of the fishing area.)
____Tools (Reel Wrench, pliers, screwdriver, file, rod varnish, etc. Something will need repairing.)
____Fillet knife (And freezer bags if bringing fish home.)
____Fannypack (For wading the reefs.)
____Backpack (If walking a long way.)
____Cooler (80-qt. if you plan to keep fish or bring them home.)
____Umbrella (Golf, to ward off rain and sun.)
____Sponge (For cleaning up.)
____Small disposable lighter (For rod tips plus epoxy, melting rope ends, lighting a candle, etc.
____Ziploc® Bags (Can be used to keep items dry.)

Other

____

____

____

____

____

Packing

I have an 80-qt. Gott® cooler that I pack full of gear. When I arrive at a destination I unpack the gear and use the cooler to hold ice, water, lunch and the fish I catch. It can also be used as a boat seat. I like the Gott because its carrying handles are built right into its walls and are very sturdy. The hasp on the cooler, however, is not made for traveling. Bolting the hasp is a good idea.

Fishing Tip: I solved the problem of holding down the lid of the Gott® cooler by, (1) drilling a hole through the wall of the cooler as well as the hasp and then (2) threading a plastic bolt (used to hold toilet seats) in the hole from inside out. When I'm through packing, I slip the hasp over the bolt and

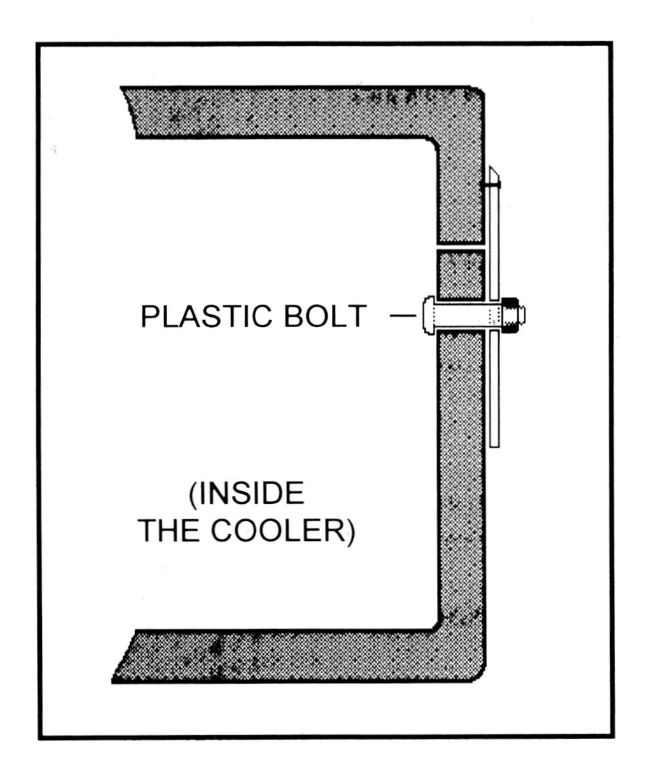

Illustration for using a plastic bolt for the hasp on an 80-qt. Gott cooler.

The cooler and everything that fits into it.

I take along an extra duffel bag. You can buy good ones at an army-navy store for less than $25. Get one with a heavy plastic zipper. If, on the way home, the cooler is needed to carry fish fillets, then everything else can be stowed in the duffel bag.

Fishing Tip: Spray canvas items like duffelbags with 3M Ultrathon® water repellent to ward off salt and moisture.

I buy reasonably large Rubbermaid® containers and pack most of my gear in these plastic boxes. In one I put all my hooks and cutting pliers (English electricians pliers have great leverage and can cut the eye of a #7 hook with ease). In another box go the lures I use. These are packed **without** hooks.

Reels, each wrapped in an old sock, go in another container. The medical supplies are packed together, and I put tools, scale, knife, pen, tape, and IGFA certificates in a zip-lock bag in another plastic box. Extra line, leader, swivels and a fingernail cutter go in another box. All these boxes go in the cooler. I pack my clothes, including rain gear, around and on top of boxes to prevent shifting. The plastic boxes have watertight lids and can be used, after unpacking, to hold maps or sandwiches, or a camera, when going out on a boat.

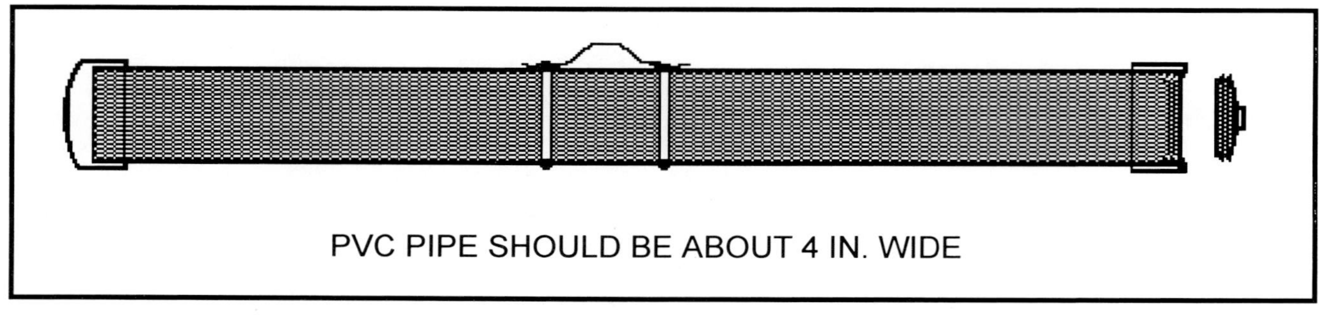

It is easy to make a sturdy rod case out of PVC pipe. The length is dictated by your longest rod section.

I have a couple of rod cases that I made out of PVC pipe. They are easy to make. Get a medium walled pipe that is sturdy but not too heavy. Choose pipe 4 to 4½ in. in diameter. Get a length of pipe that is 3 inches longer than your longest rod piece. Cap one end and glue it in place. Put a threaded plug on the other end using plastic pipe glue. I made a handle for my cases by taking two pipe clamps and a piece of old leather belt. I put the handle at the balance point after the case is loaded. These cases have lasted more than ten years.

Recently I purchased a couple of travel rods from G. Loomis®. These are 8-ft. 7-in. rods which can be broken down into four 27-in. pieces. I take one of these rods, along with a light reel and few lures in a "carry-on" bag. Then, if my main bags get lost, I can still go fishing. In the "carry-on" also goes the rest of the gear that is important: tickets, passport, change of clothes, extra glasses, sundries, and small miscellaneous items.

I usually take a swim mask and delete the fins. An umbrella and gaff go in the rod cases. My camera goes in the "carry-on" or in an extra case or bag. I therefore end up with three pieces of luggage.

Off Manono Island, Western Samoa.

The rod case and cooler are sent as baggage and the "carry-on" I carry with me.

Considerations for Extended Trips

The Specific Checklist is intended for a week's trip. It assumes accommodations will be a room in a hotel. If you intend to stay longer, that is, rent a local house or apartment, cook your own food and generally make your own way, then consider also bringing the following:

___**Disposable kitchenware.** You can buy such things at a swap meet. A used blender is great for smoothies made with local bananas, pineapple and papaya. You will need a cooking pot and forks and spoons. These can be donated when you leave.

___**Toilet paper**. In the boondocks it is scarce and usually rough.

___**A small fan**. There is usually no air conditioning in the "out of the way" places, but electricity is available. A fan can cool things off and keep mosquitos away.

___**Sheet and towels**. A sheet blanket is ideal for the cool, early mornings that occur even at the equator.

___**Packets of food:** powdered milk, chocolate milk or coffee. You can live for a week on dry cereal, fruit and milk, if necessary.

___**Woolite® and clothespins**. You can wash out quick-drying clothes by soaking them, even if there is no hot water.

___**Mosquito netting** or a yard or two of plastic screen, or both. The screen can be used to patch broken screens and is especially helpful if you are mosquito-sensitive. A small can of bug spray is useful. You close windows and doors and spray the room while out fishing. A mosquito net can be draped over a bed at night and is light enough to take along.

Possible Medical Problems

Potential medical problems that arise on South Pacific fishing trips are: (**1**) diarrhea from local food or water, (**2**) coral scratch infections, (**3**) sunburn or (**4**) insect bites or jellyfish stings.

1. For diarrhea, **Lomotil® or Imodium AD®** can work wonders for a short period of time. Obviously, however, diarrhea is best avoided. Veteran travelers always boil the water they drink or that they use when brushing their teeth or for making ice, juice or reconstituting dry milk. A large aluminum tea kettle is ideal for boiling water and having clean water ready for use all the time.

2. I have found that if a scratch is washed thoroughly with antiseptic soap, cleaned with peroxide, followed by an antiseptic cream, such as **Bacitracin®** or Bactoban® (mupirocin, generic), and then bandaged, little trouble occurs. It is difficult, however, to keep these areas dry. If you want to keep fishing, cuts or scratches should be looked at daily.

3. The best way to prevent sunburn is to use a good protecting cream with a sun protection factor of 15 or more. I find that my ankles and the back of my legs need the most protection. Experiment until you find a cream that doesn't sting your eyes or cause a skin reaction. If you do get burned, cover up when out in the sun and try to take a cold shower. Remedies such as **Solarcaine®** can be helpful.

4. For mosquito and other insect bites, **Caladryl®** seems to work well. Do not rub jellyfish stings. Wash them with fresh water and apply a baking soda paste.

Removing a Hook

Although rare, a hook stuck in the skin may surprise the reef fisherman. For a hook stuck in tight skin the rule is, if you can't free a hook after some gentle effort, grit your teeth and push it through. Then cut off the barb and slide the shank back out.

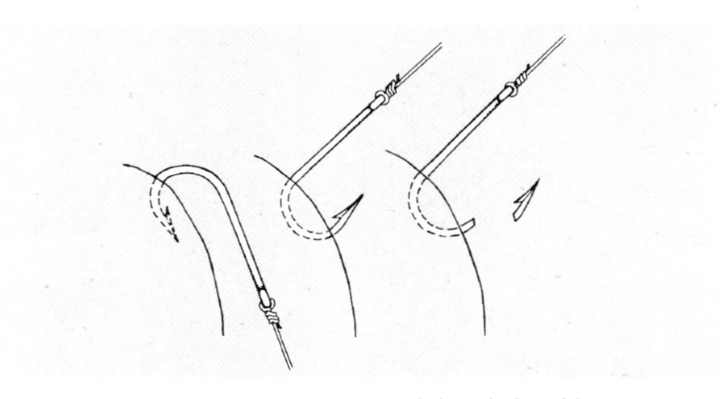

"Push-through" Method for tight skin.

In loose skin, put a loop of strong line around the curve of the hook, press firmly on the head of the hook to free the barb and snatch it out.

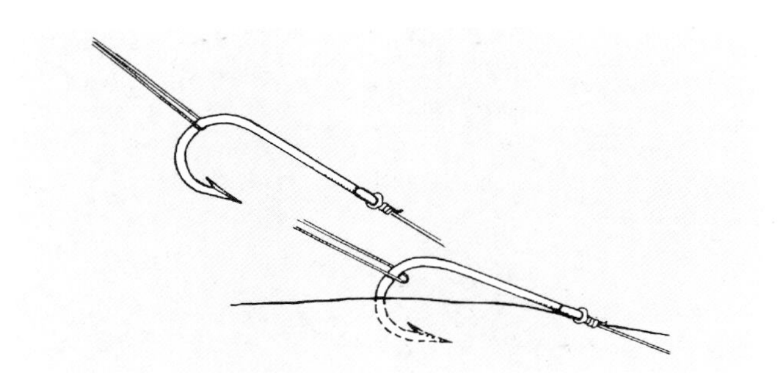

The "Standard" Method for hooks in loose skin.

Avoiding Ciguatera

If any large local snapper (*Lutjanus bohar* in particular) is offered to you as food, respectfully decline. The red-eyed snapper is notorious for carrying the ciguatera toxin. I have tested fish for ciguatera poisoning and found that many of the predatory fish, especially on reefs that have been disturbed by dredging or storms, show signs of the ciguatera toxin.

Common early symptoms of ciguatera poisoning include nausea, vomiting, diarrhea, and stomach cramps. Weak muscles and joints and pain in the extremities may follow. Sometimes there is the strange reversal of sensation where hot things

Medical Kit for Distant or Extended Trips

For expeditions to distant places you may want to consider a more extensive medical kit. I had my local doctors in Hawai'i prescribe a kit for me, and it includes the following:

Medicines*

___Aspirin or Tylenol® (For Fever or Pain.)
___Lomotil® or Imodium® or Pepto Bismol® (To control diarrhea.)
___Benadryl® (In case there is some allergic reaction to bites or stings.)
___Bacitracin® or Bactoban® (For bacterial skin infections.)
___Donnatal® (To control abdominal pain due to gastroenteritis.)
___Septra® (DS For respiratory, skin and urinary infections.)
___Vicodin® (For pain.)
___Phenergan® (For nausea.)
___Proventil® inhaler (Asthma)
___Epinephrine® (In case of allergic reactions. Is found in a bee sting kit.)
___Lotromin® (clotrimazole) cream (For fungal skin infections.)
___Cortisporn® otic (ear drops.)
___Gentamycin® ophthalmic solution (eye infections.)

Supplies*

Q.tips, Kerlex rolls, gauze, bandaids, waterproof tape, thermometer, ace wrap and peroxide should be included for minor problems. Just in case someone gets a more severe injury or as an extra safety precaution, you may wish to include: #25 1½" sutures, and needles, needle holder, a scalpel (#11 blade), forceps, scissors, latex gloves, Lidocaine®, syringe, Betadine® solution/pads and a normal saline solution (a severe cut may have to be stitched up).

All these medicines and supplies fit into a 6- by 10-inch plastic box 3 inches deep. While I take this kit with me on long trips, I have made only superficial use of it so far. Prevention is the best medicine. If you are careful about what you eat and drink and if you take reasonable precautions, such a kit will probably not have to be used.

***None of the above medicines or supplies should be used without consulting your own physician.**

feel cold and vice versa. **Mannitol**, a simple sugar IV medication has been used to treat this illness.

Until every big reef fish can be tested, avoid ingesting parts of any large reef predators such as barracuda, snapper and groupers. These larger fish prey on the smaller reef fish that eat the algae that contain the toxin. The toxin builds up in the reef predators over their lifetimes, and the bigger the fish the more likely they are to have higher concentrations of the poison.

Fish that are safe to eat are the pelagic fish: tunas, wahoo, dolphin and Spanish mackerel (walu), as well as small reef fish such as papio, small jack, wrasse or other small local fish that the natives eat and recommend. Fortunately, there is a kit now being manufactured to test for ciguatera, and this would be a good addition to your travel kit.

The Pacific red snapper (Lutjanus bohar) is a prime carrier of ciguatera toxin. Catch this great fighter and return it to the sea.

What to Take When Wading the Reef

Several years ago, my son Derek and I went fishing at Christmas Island. We had arrived in the afternoon, and in the evening we drove a Toyota wagon west to the beach, away from the main road that goes south to London. After rigging our poles, we waded out on the fingers of the shallow reef to cast beyond the swell that broke all along the coral.

On my very first cast, a bluefin trevally ('omilu) weighing more than 12 lbs. struck, ran my lure around a coral head and was gone. I had to wade back to the beach, run to the vehicle, dig out another lure, rig it and get back to my spot. Another cast, and another lure was gone!

Meanwhile, Derek had caught a 3-lb. snapper so we both ran back to the truck together. I figured that each round trip took about 15 minutes. I caught a peacock grouper on my third trip around. By then the sun was sinking on the edge of the horizon and it was time to quit for the day.

There is hardly anything more discouraging than losing a lure when "the bite is on" and not having another lure with you is especially painful when you are a long way from the home base or boat. To avoid this problem the reef wader should wear or carry the following gear:

A long, light spinning rod: I like to use a rod that is at least 9 ft. long. Effective casts can then be made even when wading in water up to your waist. A long rod allows you to maneuver fish around rocks and coral. A long rod gives you greater leverage, especially when the water is high. A long rod allows you to make casts to isolate your lure and attract fish that stay in the outer periphery of the fisherman. (For specific information, see Rods and Reels p. 26.)

Matching reel and line: The spinning reel should match and balance the rod. Sometimes you may be casting for several hours. If your reel is too heavy, you can tire quickly. New graphite reels make balancing and matching easy. The line should also match the rod and reel. A long pole is used to make long casts; but, if the line is too heavy for a small reel, no amount of trying will get the lure out to the fish. Spinning reels should have high gear ratios, at least 5- or 6-to-1. This allows a quick retrieve from long distances so that more casts can be made in a shorter time and provides an opportunity to put action on a lure that is moving, with the current, towards you.

Light cotton shirt and swim trunks or biking shorts: I always wear a light cotton shirt because I am never sure just how long I will be out in the sun. Cotton is cool and dries quickly. I like to wear shorts that are a light nylon-cotton blend. This material dries quickly and is tough. If your shorts have pockets, they should have plastic zippers or button flaps so that they don't fill with water in case you have to dive underwater to retrieve a lure or control yourself in a breaking wave.

The author is shown wading the sand flats at the southern tip of Aitutaki in the Cook islands.

Jogging shoes: After a lot of experimentation, I am convinced that a good pair of jogging shoes and heavy socks make the best combination for wading reefs. Jogging shoes are light, but their soles are very tough and have good traction. The shoes have good support. They dry quickly, and the modern plastic components seem to hold up well after being in salt water. I wear a heavy pair of white athletic socks to protect my ankles and to prevent sand from drifting down into the shoes.

Hat and sunglass: A hat should be light colored on top and dark under the visor. Any of the common fishing hats, mostly made in Korea, are good if they follow this color scheme. Polaroid glasses are also nice to have. Mine fool me all the time. I always think that it is much cooler than it really is.

Polaroids help the angler see fish when the sunlight glares off the water. People like me who wear bifocals can get Polaroid sunglasses with the correct prescription.

A long pole, light cotton shirt, and nylon cotton shorts make it easier to fish.

A good pair of walking or jogging shoes and heavy socks are excellent for wading the reefs.

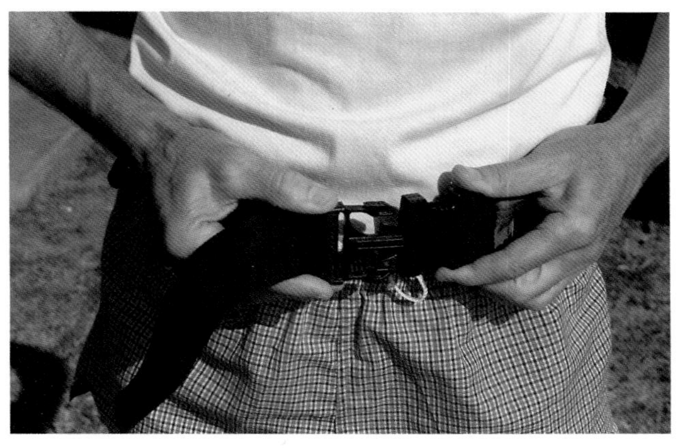

A biker's fannypack holds lures ready in plastic bags.

Fannypack: Although fannypacks are primarily sold to bike riders, I have found that they are durable and easy to get into and their plastic zippers stand up in salt water. My pack has a quick belt release, which also is plastic. I use the pack to hold extra lures, hooks, pliers and a nail clipper. The lining of the pack should be tough and smooth.

Two ways to handle lures: Prior to wading, the lures that you are going to use should be preassembled and placed in heavy plastic bags (2.75 ml. plastic sandwich bags will do). I usually take about six lures with 80-lb. test soft monofilament leaders and swivels pre-tied. Package one lure to a bag. This way the hooks never get entangled with each other. I drop a lure in a bag and then loosely push the leader in on top. When I need a lure, it comes out with the least amount of fuss.

An alternative is to store the lures and hooks separately. Put pre-cut treble hooks in a plastic bag or plastic box and store the lures loosely in the fannypack. Use pliers to bend the hooks on the lures as needed. I use this second method of handling lures because I have learned to do it quickly and no pre-preparation is needed.

Net or gaff (optional) and fish line: I used to think that a small hand gaff was a necessity. If your fish is big or toothy (like a barracuda) and you want to keep it, then a gaff is helpful. If you are going to keep the fish, gaffing it in the head allows for better control and assures that it won't be lost in the rocks. For the past five years, however, I have not needed a gaff or a net. Instead, I have tried to play the fish longer. Unless it was a trophy fish or wanted for supper that night, I have released it after the battle, using a pair of pliers to pull out the lure.

A net assures that the fish can live if it is released. Almost every time, however, the hooks from the lure get entangled in the net and the snag takes time to unravel. The net also can be awkward to carry. A holder on the fannypack that allows the gaff or net to trail behind your back is an effective way to keep them handy.

A fish line is used to keep fish alive and fresh in the water until you can get them to a cooler. It is also handy for dragging larger fish in the water a long way back to home base. Fish lines are usually 10 ft. of ¼-in. nylon. Some lines come ready-made with a sharp brass ferrule on one end. Pass the ferrule through the soft skin of the fish's bottom jaw, and tie it off. You can also tie a uni-knot (a slip knot) around the fish's tail. I have continued to fish with as many as three big fish tied on one line. If there is any current or wave action, however, the tethered fish can reduce your mobility.

A belt gimbals (optional): A gimbals to support the rod butt is not a necessity, and each fisherman must decide how much gear he is willing to carry around. If, however, the fish are big (over 10 pounds), a gimbals is really nice to have available.

A Word About Boats

More than half the time you go spinning, you will need a boat to reach the reef. If the lagoon is deep and you can't wade to the coral shelf, any kind of skiff, punt or canoe will do to get you there. In such cases you take the same gear you would take when wading the reef plus a cooler to be left with the skiff.

If the local boat has an outboard motor and the reef is a long way from shore, make sure there are some paddles and an anchor aboard. Always take plenty of water on a boat trip. The sun is high in the South Pacific, and you can get dehydrated.

It is helpful to bring your tools with you to help with repairs that might be required. I find that the most frequent problem with outboard motors is that water gets mixed with the fuel. Storage containers and delivery systems in the Pacific are marginal, and this probably contributes to such difficulties.

In an open boat, a golf umbrella is useful to hide behind when running in a sudden rainstorm or as a sun protector when you are sitting in the boat eating lunch. Some fruit and candy are also nice to bring along.

The best boat from which I have spun a lure was an open double-bottomed 27-ft. Yamaha. The inside deck was easy to stand on, and the boat was long enough so that three people could whip (cast) at the same time. This long skiff had two outboard motors. One big motor got us around and the smaller one was used for maneuvering along the reef's edge. In general, dive boats make good platforms for spinning.

With long poles and heavier lures, it is possible to spin almost any reef from the outside on a nice day. You need a big boat, but one that can get close to the wave break and then out again if necessary. Fishing from the outside increases your chances of landing a big fish because a big fish running up or down the reef does not endanger the line like it would if you were spinning from shore. In addition, the fish can be backed to deeper water and pumped up free of the coral.

One technique I have pioneered involves moving slowly along the edge of the outside reef casting 1- to 3-oz. popping lures into the break and dragging them off the reef toward the deep alley at the edge of the blue water. You may have to carefully describe to local captains or pilots what it is you want to do, because in many cases they have never gone topwater spinning before. They will assume you simply want to troll.

A 27-ft. Yamaha Skiff, off Sapuwik Island in Pohnpei, is an ideal platform for spinning.

If you go outside the reef, try to take a boat that has two working motors. In many cases, however, you just have to take what is available and be prudent in its use. If it is a small boat, the fishing party may have to take turns spinning from the bow and stern or be content to find a spot inside the lagoon where everyone can wade to the reef's edge.

Most local boats will **not** have radios. I have experimented with CB radios and you need one with at least five watts of transmitting power. The price is coming down everyday and sometimes when I'm a mile or two out I wish I had a pair, one on the beach and one in the boat. They are, however, more of a luxury than a necessity.

Fishing Tip: Take packets of Gatorade, mix them with water and freeze them in plastic containers the night before you go fishing. Quench your thirst as it thaws the next day.

The thick lip or yellow spot trevally is a good fighter.

THE TACKLE

I fish artificial surface lures 90 to 95 percent of the time. Almost every fish featured in this book was caught on an artificial lure. Almost every fish pictured was caught on a lure that I made myself.

I fish topwater poppers because most reef predators are attracted to bait fish on the surface. Surface bait such as flying fish, halfbeaks, reef mullet, sardines, wrasse, tangs, and damsel fish congregate on or near the surface of the water. The eyes of trevally, snapper, and barracuda are set so they can see up as well as forward. These predators can actually track a lure in the air. That is why many strikes are made within two or three seconds after the lure hits the water. In the early days at Christmas Island, inside the big lagoon, I had a 6-lb. white trevally intercept a lure in the air!

The attack rate for surface lures is very high. A surface lure does not hang up on the coral, which may lie just below the surface. Sinking lures can be used, but they must be picked up quickly after the cast in order to avoid snagging them in the coral. Topwater lures provide the added bonus of allowing the angler to see every pass made at the artificial bait. It is, therefore, easier to tell whether or not there are any fish in the area.

Rods

Spinning rods for fishing the coral reef need to be light and long. Famous island fisherman Warren Ackerman uses Orvis graphite steelhead rods. They are light, strong and ten feet long. In Costa Rica, Warren has caught tarpon weighing over 50 lbs. with these rods. The rods work for Pacific reef fish just as well. They can handle from 4- to 20-lb. test line and stand up to big trevally.

I use graphite rods and rod blanks from G. Loomis® Inc. of Woodland, Washington. G. Loomis has IMX, IM6 and Premier classes of rods. Each time a lighter, stronger composite comes along, I try it out and each time I like the rod better. So now I use a 10-foot IM6 blank with a moderately fast action (the bend is mostly in the tip). IM6 is 20 percent lighter than regular graphite. I use large, ceramic single-foot guides with a larger than average tip so that I can reel a knot that ties the leader to the line right up into the guides.

My reel seats are conventional FUJI FPS 20, 22 and 24 fitted to the blanks. I like a cork butt because it is easier on your hands and allows the rod to float if you drop it over the side or lose it in the surf. With a rod like this and a light matching graphite reel, I can cast all day long without getting tired.

I can't impress upon sport fishermen enough that to catch the big one their rods should be

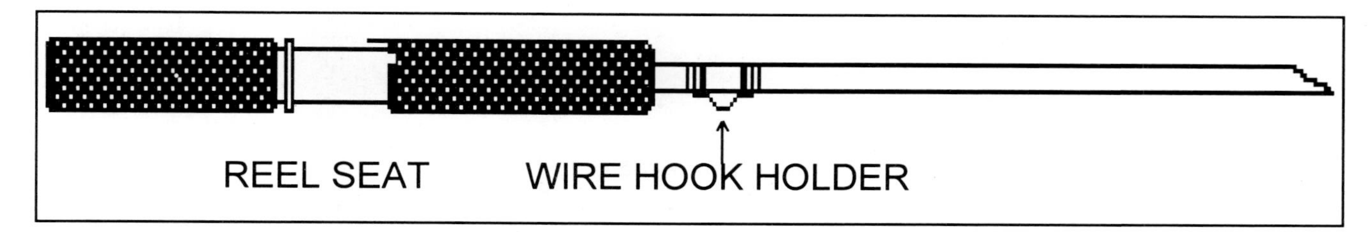

No. 23 stainless wire can be twisted and then wrapped near the butt of the pole to hold the lure's hook.

long. The minimum effective length is 8½ feet. Try to have a moderately fast taper; i.e., a rod that bends more at the tip than throughout the rod. A moderately fast taper allows for longer and more accurate casts and quicker hookups, and gives the hooked fish less time to duck into the rocks.

Although guaranteed for life, the Orvis and G. Loomis rods are very expensive. A good rod can be found in most sporting goods stores for less than half their price. However, before you buy a rod in a store, put the reel you want to use on the rod and make believe you are casting—at least 10 times. Many less-expensive rods are not balanced and this test should reveal any problems. Off-the-shelf rods are usually "butt-heavy" so try to find one that is balanced with the reel in place. You can also look in catalogs like *Cabelas* for long rods, which are already "made up."

Fishing tip: Some single-foot steel guides can rust. Run a thin layer of super glue around both sides of the collar that holds the ceramic donut to form a seal. Wash guides with fresh water and wax after each trip.

Generally, the heavier the lure and line, the stiffer the rod needs to be. When I first started spinning the reefs, I used a lure that weighed approximately 1 ounce. Then I started making lures that were bigger and weighed 2 and 3 oz. I found that my old rods were too flexible to control the added weight. Now I fit my poles, line and reels to the lure that I want to use, and I take several different sizes of poles, line and lures with me.

I have recently purchased a couple of 4-piece IM6 traveling rods. The rods are 8 ft. 7 in. long when put together, yet each piece is no more than 27 in. long and can easily fit in the overhead rack of a jet. I like this rod for light spinning, trying to catch big fish on 6- and 8-lb. test line. It is also a safety valve. Because I carry it with me (and a light reel and a few lures as well), I know that I will always be able to go fishing even if the airline misplaces my other baggage.

Even though I'm not high on trolling, it is sometimes useful to drag a lure in the water when moving, in deeper water, from one spot to the next. For this I use a standup 6-foot Stroker rod by Sabre, with a conventional Penn Senator® 113 HLW or Penn Jigmaster® reel filled with 20-pound test line.

Sometimes a trolled lure can be productive if conditions are right. When traveling between reefs, watch for birds or sticks or logs. Here a mahi'mahi (dolphin) was hiding under a log.

I remember a time off the east coast of Pohnpei, we were running back to a warm shower and a hot meal when our guide, Peter Arthur, spotted a floating stick. Dolphinfish, the Pacific's mahi'mahi, like to hang around floating objects that attract small bait fish. Sure enough, several of these beautiful blue-green and yellow fish were in the vicinity. I quickly rigged an orange-pink plug on my stroker rod and after one pass we were off to the races. A conventional 3/0 or 4/0 reel, a light boating rod and light spinning gear can be useful additions to three different weight long rods and different-sized spinning reels.

Reels

Reels are getting better all the time, primarily because new breakthroughs in materials are permitting manufacturers to make them lighter by incorporating graphite housings around the gears. I generally use Penn reels because their construction is sturdy. Their internal gears are stainless steel and rarely break down. I use the Penn 550SS and 650SS most of the time. Occasionally I use the 750SS reel when throwing super big lures a long way with 20-and 30-lb. test line. Penn also has a graphite 5500SS reel, which I use with my light travel rod.

But Penn reels have their drawbacks. The rate of retrieve on the 550 reels is too slow to compensate for spinning off a moving boat or when the tide is coming at you. In these cases I turn to the Shimano TSS-3, whose spool is fairly large and whose gear ratio is almost 6-to-1.

On the smaller reels I use 8- and 12-lb. test line; on the 650, I use 16- and 20-lb. test line; on the TSS-3 I use 16-lb. test line, and on the 750 I use 30-lb. test line. I have never found it necessary to use larger rigs.

There are other good reels. New innovations in reel design taper the spools. They wrap the line on the spool in different ways to produce longer and smoother casts. Of the newer reels, I like Shimano's Stradic® ST4000F with a 6.2-to-1 gear ratio. I have also used Orvis, Mitchell, and Garcia Cardinal® reels for years, but the smaller reels now being made are not rugged enough to handle the reef predators of the South Pacific. Some reels come equipped with a line holder, but most spools lack a means of handling the loose end of the line. One way to handle the problem is to use a velcro® cloth fastener. You can write the reel and line size on the cloth with a permanent marker.

Line

The line strength you adopt depends on your objectives. The lighter the line, the farther the

If you go for records, then the line strength must be accurate. A yellowfin tuna caught inside the reef at Pohnpei on a super LOLO lure.

cast and the more limber the pole should be. I like to fish 6-, 8-, 12-, 16- and 20-lb. test line because these are line class sizes recognized by the International Game Fish Association (IGFA). If a record fish is caught, the line I use will be the accurate maximum strength for a particular category.

Different brands of line may vary considerably. Ande Tournament® line appears to be classified very accurately but I notice that it must be replaced frequently. Maxima is soft, but seems to break above its designated line strength. I have tried using Trilene line, but its classification is strange for U.S. anglers since it is measured in kilograms. Eight-kg. test line is actually 17.8 lbs. of breaking strength.

Very strong and extremely thin braided line, such as Fenwick's Iron Thread®, is now available. You should be able to cast 30-lb. line a mile because the line is so light. Special care is needed in using these kevlar lines, especially in tying secure knots. I believe that this line might make good leaders, as it is light, thin, and strong.

Trilene line, when it was first introduced, was paying $1,000 for a world record. I was using their line in hopes of paying for one of my fishing trips. I caught a 14-lb. bluefin trevally on 8-kg. test line and entered it in the 16-lb. line class. The IGFA wrote back and told me that the line tested out in 20-lb. class. From then on I strictly used Ande Tournament line. Eighty and 100-lb. test **J®** line makes great leader material because J line is soft, pliable and small in diameter.

Fishing Tip: If your monofilament line gets twisted from a lure that spins or from spooling it on incorrectly, you can make it lose its memory by soaking the spool in fairly warm water.

Fishing tip: You can test your knots and line strength at the same time. Tie one end of the scale firmly to a high support and tie your line to the hook end of the scale. Let the line hang straight down. Put on a pair of gloves and wrap the line around your gloved hand. Have a friend note the weight as you slowly pull down on the line You can estimate within a quarter of a pound the breaking strength of the line this way. Check to see if the line breaks at the knot. If not, practice retying until the line breaks above the knot

Checking Your Line Strength: One way to get an accurate estimate of the strength of your line is to try it out on a good spring scale. Chatillion makes quite accurate spring scales. These scales can also be used for the accurate weighing of fish if they are tested before your trip.

Gaffs and Nets

Gaffs: Veteran fisherman know that most gaffs are too large for the fish that are brought alongside. When we see poor gaffing, the problem is not only a matter of inexperience. It occurs because the mate has the wrong instrument in his hands. Ordinarily, the gaff opening should be equal to the width of the fish it is used on. This means that a standard #12 stainless steel hook, with an opening of about 2 in., could be used to gaff 97 percent of the fish that are "hooked up".

A smaller opening means that fish will not fall in the space between the shaft and point of the gaff, but will be impaled almost every time. A smaller hook is also easier to maneuver. Tony Stormont, my Florida "Top Hook" connection, uses a #12 stainless hook (with the barb flattened)

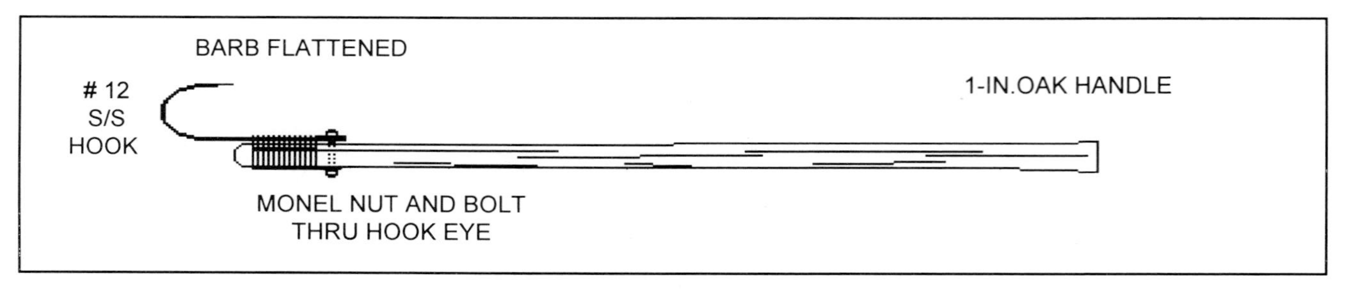

It is easy to make a gaff using an axe or hoe handle and a No. 12 stainless hook.

fastened to an axe handle. He usually gaffs large king mackerel, but once he gaffed a green 70-lb. wahoo with this small-sized gaff. While that feat is exceptional, any fish up to 50 lbs. should be handled easily with this type of gaff.

To make an efficient gaff, use a one-inch diameter oak hoe handle 4 ft. long or a small axe handle from the local hardware store. These handles becomes wider at the end, making gripping easier. Take a #12 Mustad stainless hook and pound the barb flat. Then cut a groove in the narrow end of the handle to fit the shank of the hook. (A Dremel® tool does this easily, but you could use a drill or a drill wrapped with sandpaper.) Two inches from the end of the handle, drill a 3/16-in. hole and countersunk above the hole to fit the eye of the hook. Pass a 3/16-in. stainless bolt, 1¼ in. long, and pass this through the eye to hold the hook in place. Then wrap some soft stainless wire around the hook and the handle to keep the hook from moving.

The wrapping proceeds by taking one end, laying it along the axis of the handle and wrapping over this end. The wrap starts from the hook end of the handle and proceeds back toward the eye. When the eye is reached, take two turns around the loose bolt. Then the nut is turned tightly on the bolt to hold the wire in place. A few taps with a hammer on the nut end of the bolt prevents the nut from coming loose. A quicker solution to a wire wrap is to use a small stainless steel hose clamp you can purchase at any auto parts shop.

I have used this gaff with great success all over the Pacific. Mine is now over 15 years old and still useful. This gaff also packs well in a rod case because of its smaller hook. A short hand gaff can be made the same way. Just cut down on the length of the handle. A 4-ft. gaff, however, is often needed because you may be fishing from a boat that is several feet above the water.

Before I became conservation-minded I gaffed almost every fish. Now, however, I gaff only occasionally because I want the choice of being able to release the fish if it is full of roe or if it is not needed or wanted for food. Some fish like barracuda, walu, and wahoo have very sharp teeth and need to be handled carefully. In this case, a gaff

Derek Dunn-Rankin and a nice snapper caught off Christmas Island, Kiribati (note axe handle gaff).

is handy. Barracuda should be lip-gaffed so that they can be released. Walu and wahoo are prized pelagic food fish and are rarely released.

Nets: If you do not wish to injure the fish, then a good net with a long handle is useful. Although the hooks may get caught in the net, you can usually release the fish unharmed. The problem is that it is difficult to cart such a big net along on a trip. There are some collapsible nets with aluminum handles that might do the job. I find it easier, however, to play the fish a little longer and grab the tail with a gloved hand when the fish slides to the surface.

Lures

I particularly like PILI® lures. A PILI lure is designed to float tail slightly down. As it is pulled in, the lure pops the water in front of it and, during a pause, sits back on its tail. The PILI lure is effective for catching papio(trevally under 10 pounds). The lure is made of cast resin and urethane. Like a surfboard, the PILI can crack if it hits a rock. PILI lures are sold in most fishing stores in Hawai'i. PILIs can be cast or trolled. The PILI weighs a little over an ounce and can be used effectively with 8-, 10- and 12-lb. test line.

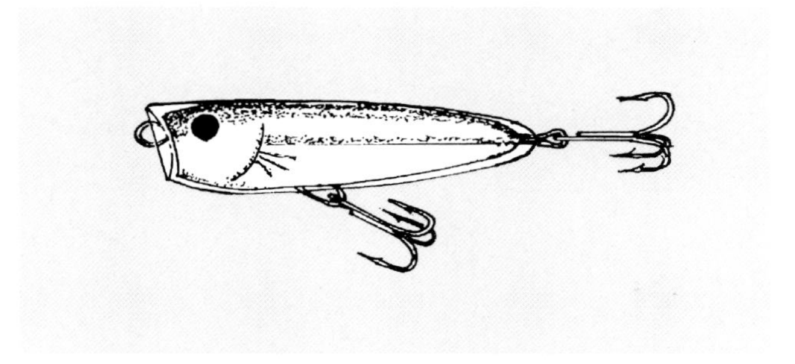

The PILI was the first successful lure that the author invented. It is now made by another company.

Tad Nottage caught two bluefin trevally on one original PILI lure off the island of Kaho'olawe, Hawai'i.

I make all the lures that I fish with, so, naturally, I think they are the best. "Making the World's Best Surface Lure" in the next chapter shows how you can make your own best lures.

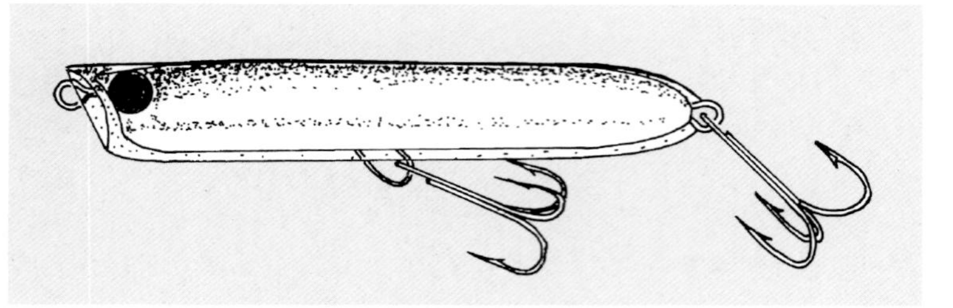

Even though the MULI and LOLO are not presently available commercially, they are pictured so that the enterprising fisherman can make his own.

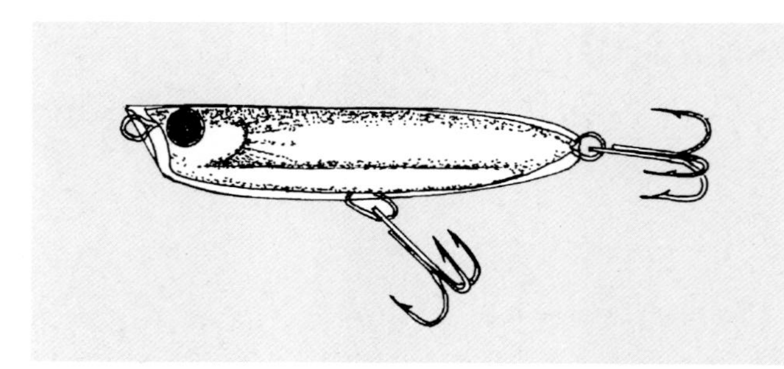

The MULI is pictured so that it can be copied.

This 17-lb. bluefin trevally couldn't resist a topwater MULI® lure. It was caught off the south coast of the big island of Hawai'i by Deighton Emmons.

I now make two different urethane core lures that vary from 6 to 8 in. long and weigh from 1½ to 3 oz. I call these new lures the MULI lure and the super LOLO lure. These lures are designed to float upright so that they do not spin when retrieved.

What I like best about the latest lures I have made is that, with slight changes in the action of the rod tip, the lure can be made to pop or spray water, skip on the surface or jump back and forth across the line of retrieval. If the angler simply reels in the lure, some action will occur; but the MULI allows the proficient angler to make it dance.

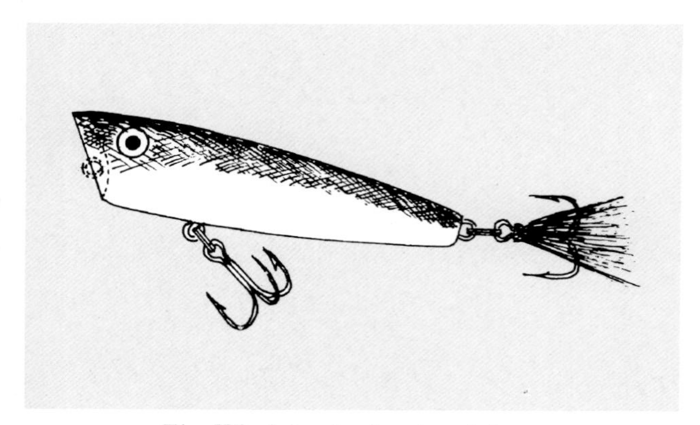

The Windcheater is a tough lure. It takes a lot of abuse but is tiring to use all day

The large 4- to 5-in. Rebel Windcheater is a good, tough topwater lure. Its front loop for attaching the line is placed well below the horizontal axis so that on retrieval the lure digs in as it pops. Its shape makes it dart from side to side. This lure is difficult to throw all day, because pulling it in is tiring and requires a stiffer, heavier pole to impart action. One advantage of the big windcheater is that it can stand a lot of abuse from accidents like hitting rocks or taking bites from sharp teeth.

Some anglers have had success with Gibb's Pencil Popper. This is a big lure that creates a large splash when it hits the surface. It is sometimes attractive to giant trevally. The lure is skipped over the surface of the water like a frightened needlefish or flying fish.

The lure you use dictates the kind of action that can be achieved. Rapala lures are diving lures with a "built-in" action. They are excellent for trolling along the edge of the reef. They are not productive, however, when casting over the reef because they will dig in and hook to the coral under the surface. Their retrieval cannot be varied. It is possible, however, to adapt the Rapala for topwater casting by removing the metal diving plane.

The old wooden Zara Spook lure by Heddon and the Scudder by Arbogast are good topwater baits for trevally. The newer plastic Spook, however, is not effective. The old spook darts from side to side in a natural way but doesn't create enough splashing to effectively attract the largest fish. The Scudder makes a big commotion on the surface when it is retrieved with long pulls, but has a tendency to roll. The Dillinger is a good lure, but its hooks and eyes are too light for the action on the Pacific reefs.

The Kastmaster is a heavy, metal spoon that seems to be the best metal lure for fishing in the South Pacific. It can be thrown a long way and is effective for trolling. Because it is heavy, the Kastmaster must be retrieved immediately to prevent it from sinking into the reef.

Kona Head lures are used strictly for trolling and you may wish to include two or three

The pencil popper is popular; it takes a fast retrieve. Stan Wright shows off his popper.

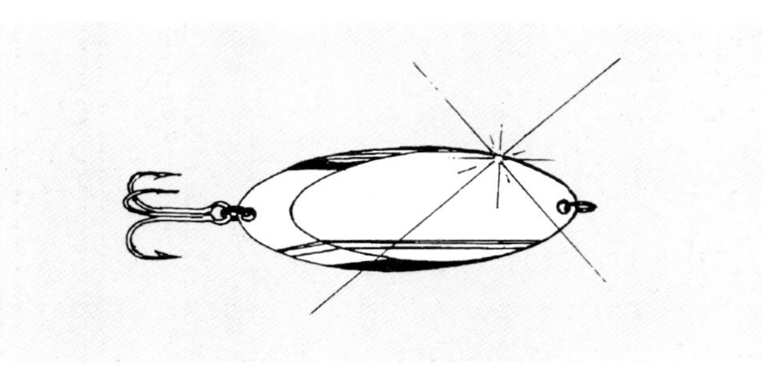

The Kastmaster has the weight to be thrown a long way.

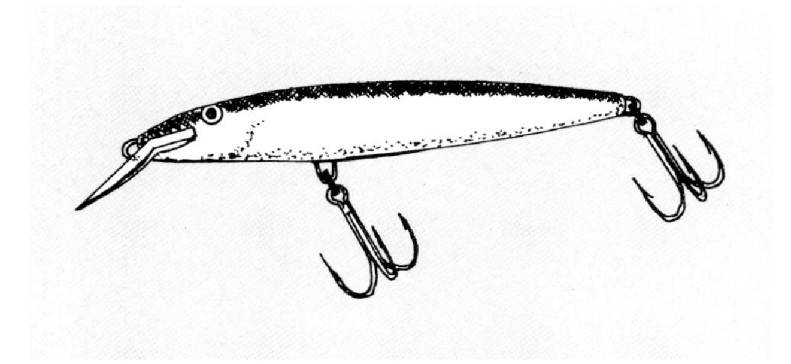

The Rapala is the best trolling artificial bait but it is tough to use over the reef because it digs in and gets caught on the coral.

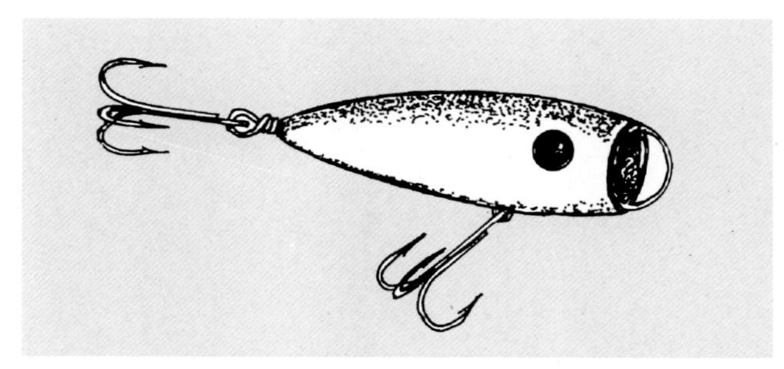

The Scudder by Arbogast is still a good lure for the reef. It has, however, a tendency to roll. Use it with a swivel.

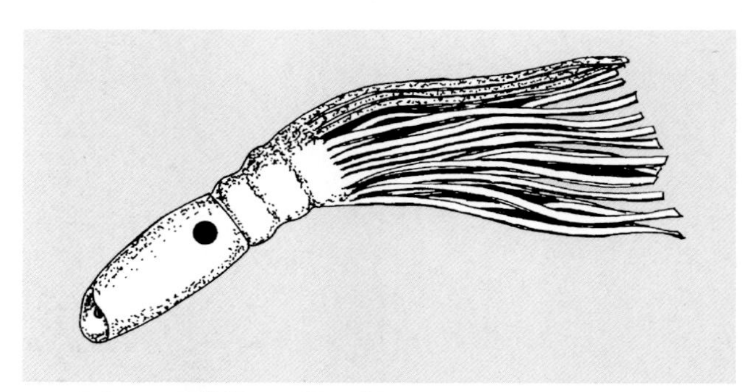

A few small Kona Heads are useful when trolling between islands. The one pictured is made out of porcelain and was invented by the author.

smaller ones for use when traveling between spots. I have found an all-white head with blue, pink, and white skirts mixed together to be most effective. This lure has been used successfully in the Bahamas to catch ono (wahoo) Tropical Clay of Hawai'i makes a porcelain white head that is a real winner.

Tout lures seem to have universal appeal. Touts work well for smaller fish because they emulate the jumping jacks that inhabit the tidal

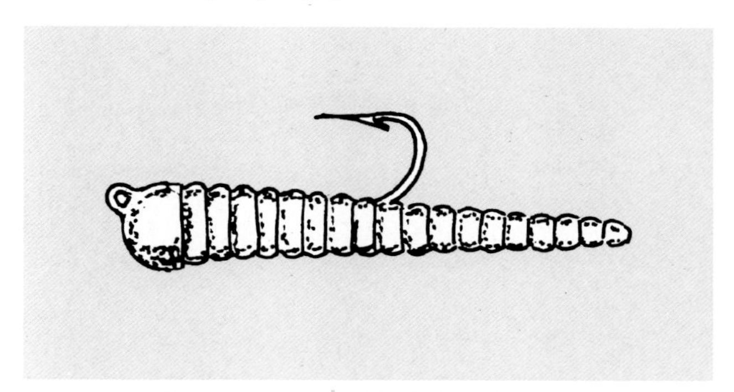

Touts can resemble local bait fish. They can work wonders on small trevally.

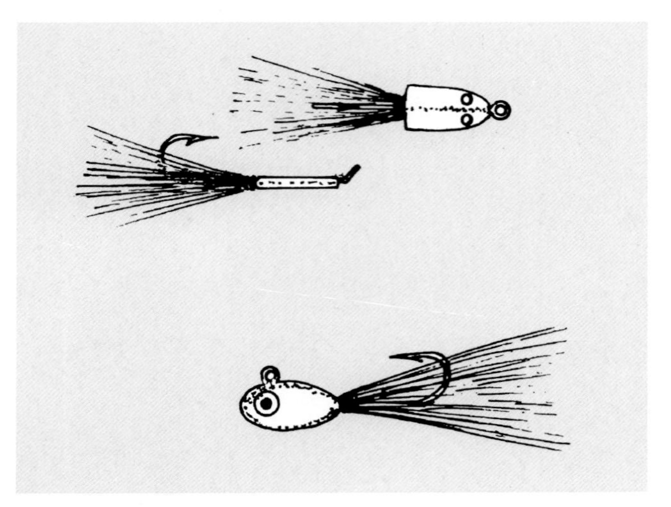

The yellow bucktail is not used much in the Pacific. It should work well, however, on grass and sand flats near the reef.

pools of the Pacific high islands or the bait fish of the coral atolls. These leadheaded jigs can be tied directly to the line because they do not spin. Black touts produce well in Hawai'i and Samoa, where black basalt cliffs, black rocks and black gobies abound. Red-headed glow touts work wonders on small reef fish such as moana, wrasse and papio.

When I fished in Florida, I hardly ever used anything but a bucktail jig. Yellow bucktails fished on the flats behind Baker's Haulover caught pompano, jack and blue runner. In the Bahamas, bucktails caught mangrove and yellowtail snapper, horse-eye jack, bar jack, cero mackerel and an occasional bonefish. A bucktail jig is a great lure but it is always tough to fish a sinking lure over coral. I have had success catching small fish, however, by throwing it to the edge of coral outcroppings in shallow, sandy areas.

You may find lures that can substitute for those I've described here. There are several PILI imitators in Hawai'i but few lures contain a core that makes them float upright even without hooks. It is a good idea to drop a surface popper in a bucket of water and observe how it floats. If turned on its side, does it pop right back up? If not, try another lure.

HOW TO MAKE THE WORLD'S BEST SURFACE LURE

If you are a serious fisherman and handy with wood and plastic, you can also enjoy the thrill of making the world's best lure of your own design and workmanship. While the process takes some time, the lures you create can be better and less expensive than any you can buy.

Internal core lures are made with two parts: **First,** a urethane core is made that contains the wire to hold the hooks and line (urethane is the material that is used to make surfboards). **Secondly,** a resin casting gives the lure its distinct shape. The resin is cast into a mold that contains the core.

Internal core lures have three distinct advantages. The first is that the lure floats upright. If tilted, it pops back to its original position. This makes it "swim" naturally and allows the lure to be used without a swivel. Next, the urethane core mimics the air bladder of a natural bait. The lure's resonance in the water is like that of a true bait fish. Finally, the inner core can be painted a variety of colors that will not fade or wash away.

Steps in Making an Internal Core Lure

1. Create a wooden stick lure that will act as a model. The wooden model should have all the characteristics that you like. Stick lures, for

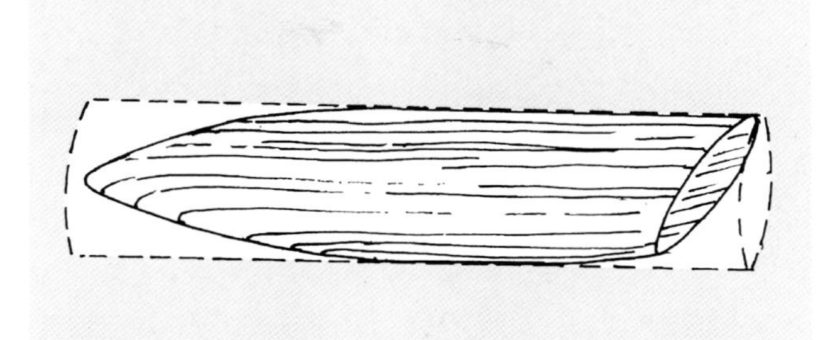

First a model is made.

example, are easy to make. Cut, shape and sand a wooden dowel. Spray-paint the wooden plug and fit it with screw eyes and hooks. Many fishermen stop at this point and use such broomstick lures as a major topwater lure. Unfortunately, stick lures, although sometimes effective, lack the brilliant permanent colors and float capabilities of urethane core resin lures, as well as the strength of an internal wire to hold the hooks.

Next, try out your wooden prototype and change or modify it until you feel it is good enough to be duplicated. It is important to have someone else use the prototype while you watch what happens. I have made as many as five different wooden models before proceeding to make a mold. Wooden lures that perform well in practice usually translate into plastic and foam with better-than-average results.

Once you have decided on the model, make a mold of it by following the illustrated steps.

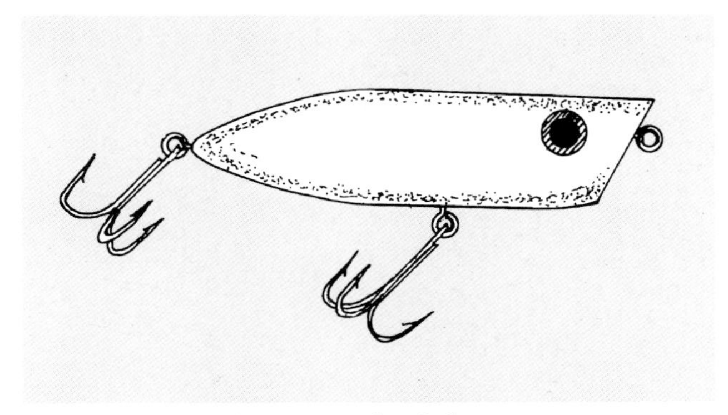

A prototype is tried out.

2. A plastic box is required to hold the rubbery compound (silastic) that will become the mold. Use pieces of clear 3/16-in. acrylic plastic to construct the box that will hold the mold. This is because silastic does not stick to smooth plastic. Usually the box is 2 to 3 in. deep, 2 to 3 in. wide and 2 to 3 in. longer than the wooden prototype.

Cut the plastic box pieces with a fine saw and hold them together with small touches of super glue (cyranoacrylate).

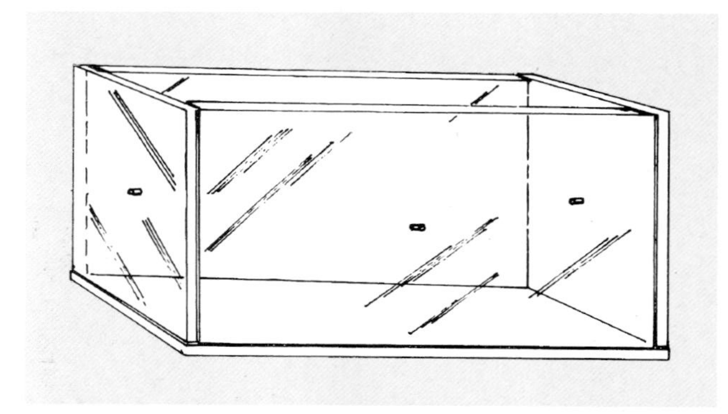

A plastic box will not stick to the mold material

Remove the hooks and eyes from the wooden model and fine-sand with #600 grit sandpaper. Rub and polish it with paste wax.

3. Drill small (1/32-in.) holes in the center of the ends and one side of the box. These holes are used to receive short lengths of stiff wire (#22 or #23 stainless leader) which are passed through the holes in the box and pushed into the screw holes of the wooden model. Here they serve to hold the model in position on its side.

4. Fill the box almost half-full with Dow-Corning 3120 silicone rubber (red) mixed with one-tenth catalyst by weight. You can get silicone rubber from fiberglass outlets. Silicone rubber is messy stuff, so use "throw away" containers to mix it in. Red silastic is hard to mix but it sets up much

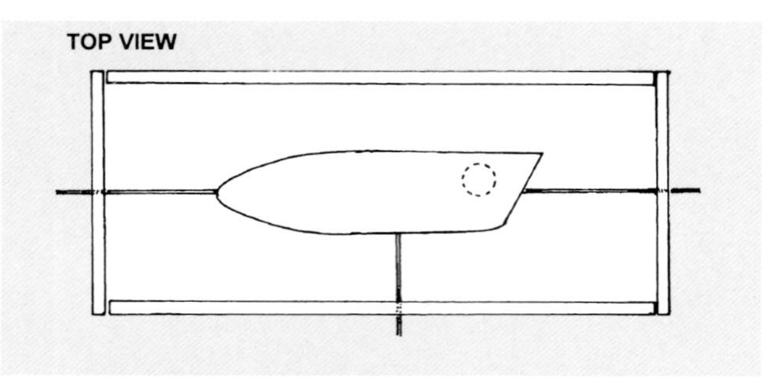

The model is held in the box by stiff wires.

tougher than white silastic. Sharply bump the container of mixed rubber against the floor in order to remove as many air bubbles as possible. Bubbles are the toughest problem to lick in creating smooth lures. If a vacuum pump and jar are available they should be used to pull the bubbles out of the silastic before pouring the mold. My son, Derek, suggests using a modified car cylinder vacuum pump to pull the air out of the plastic or converting an old refrigerator pump for the same purpose.

Place the wooden lure carefully on its side so that exactly half lies exposed. Push stiff wires (#23 stainless) into the eye holes to hold the model in place. If more silastic is needed so that exactly one-half of the stick lure is exposed, it should be added at this time.

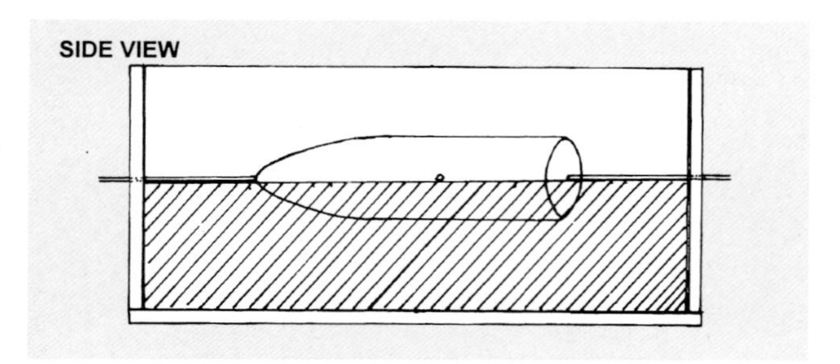

The box is filled exactly half full of silastic.

5. When the first half of the mold has hardened, (in 12 to 24 hrs.), carve four positioning holes in the rubber surface and remove the wire holding pins. The positioning holes can be cut with a sharp knife as shown. The holes do not have to be deep but should be vee shaped or conic.

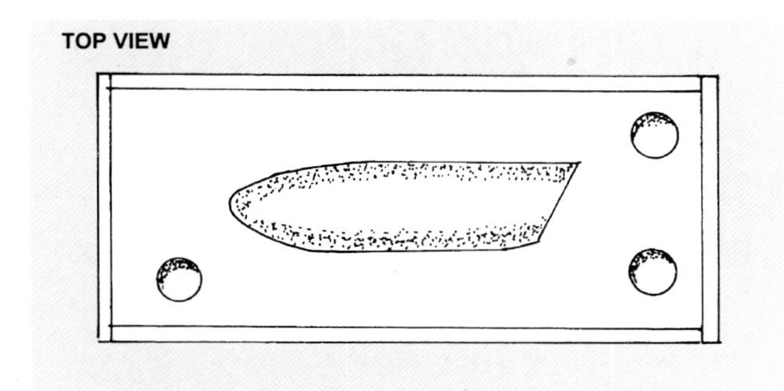

Positioning holes are cut into the hardened surface of the first half of the mold.

Next coat and rub the surface of the hardened silastic and embedded lure with paste wax. Then sprinkle baby powder over the surface and blow away the excess, leaving a light film of dust. Mix a new batch of silastic rubber and poured it over the exposed side of the wooden model. When this has hardened, break the box apart and remove the wooden prototype, leaving two mold halves.

6. Cut the tail end of the mold as shown to make a pouring hole for the casting resin. Be sure to leave room at the tail of the mold for the tail eye

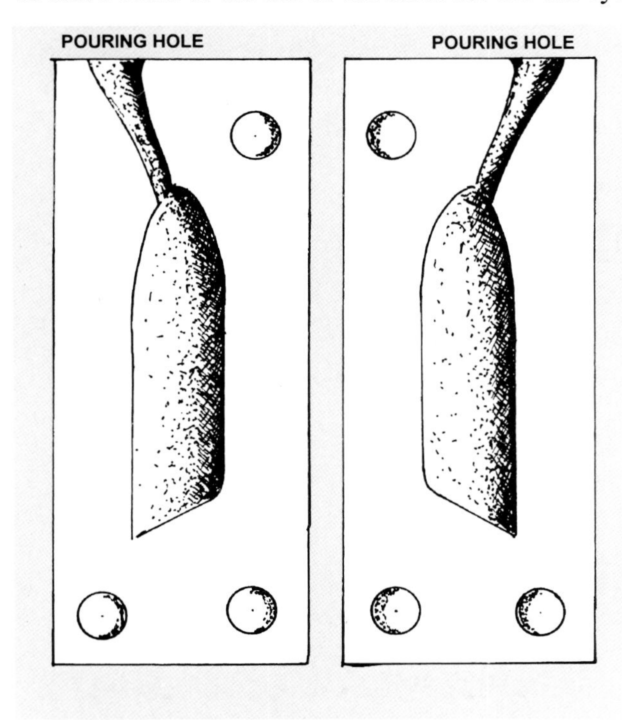

A pouring cut is made in tail end of each half.

of your wire to rest on. Once a good mold is made, it should last for making more than a 1,000 lures.

7. Make a hand jig for bending the wire, driving two 3/16-in. diameter nails into a piece of 2 x 4 wood just 1/32 in. apart. The nail heads are filed off and the nails are exposed above the surface of the board from 3/16 to ¼ in.. The block is placed in a vise and the wire is bent around one or both of the nails to start the eyeloops (also see p. 44).

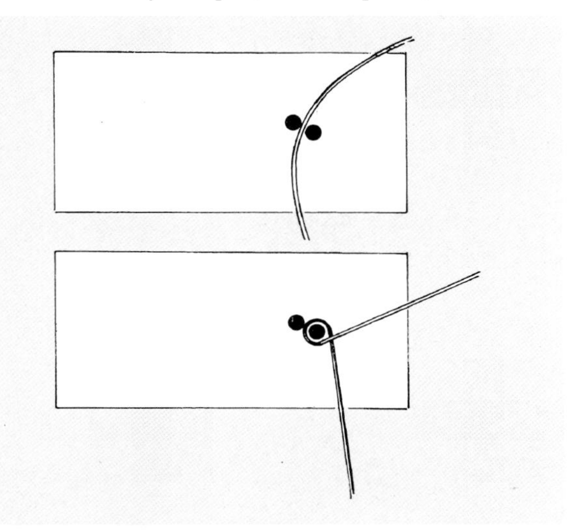

A jig or a nail in a vise is used in bending the wire.

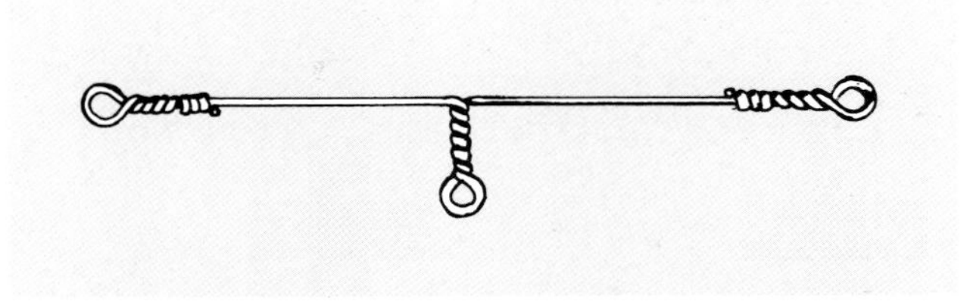

An internal wire is made using #22 stainless. A visegrip pliers is useful to hold the eye.

8. Bend #22 stainless wire to create the line and hook eyes of the lure and to stablize the core.

9. Next, make a urethane core by cutting and shaping the material that is used for surfboard cores, that is, a light urethane with a density of 4 to 5 lbs. per square inch. This urethane can be obtained from Clark Foam, Hawai'i or from pieces of foam thrown away by most surfboard shops.

Make the core all around 1/8 in. smaller than the cavity of the mold. Make a deep cut in the bottom of the core with a fine hacksaw, and insert the bent wire.

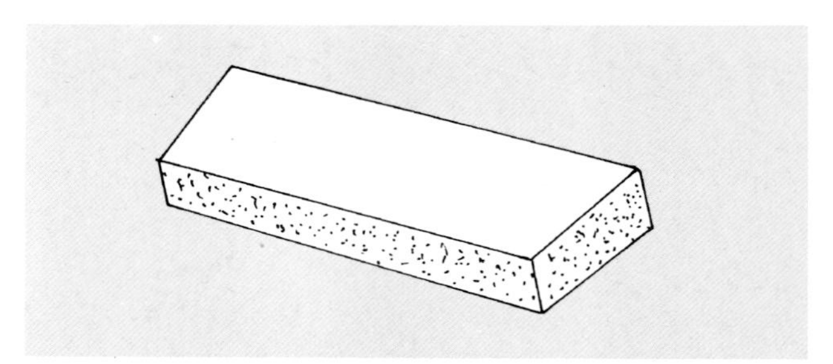

A rough urethane core is shaped with a knife and sandpaper.

10. Apply super glue to the cut, and use a vise to press the base of the urethane core together over the wire. I have found that the new heavier viscosity Jet Glue is very effective because it dries quickly. A quick-set spray is also good to use.

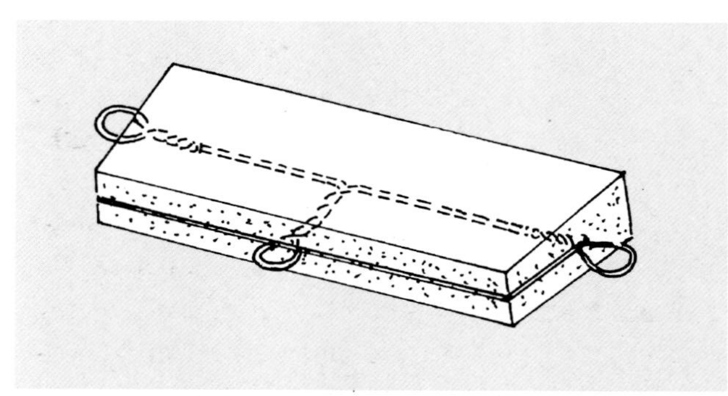

A cut is made in the core to receive the wire.

The bottom of the core is pressed together in order to hold the wire and because more casting

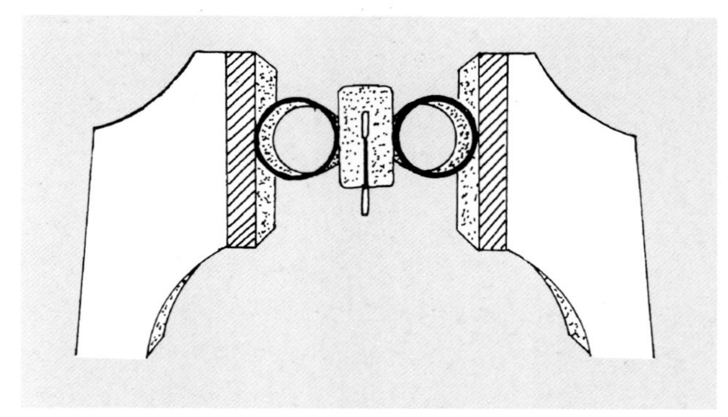

Super Glue is applied and the core and wire are pressed together in a vise.

resin will then be on the bottom of the lure, making that part heavier. A good lure should float upright without hooks. The closer the core is to the top or back of the lure, the better the lure will act in the water. Sand the finished core to shape and fit.

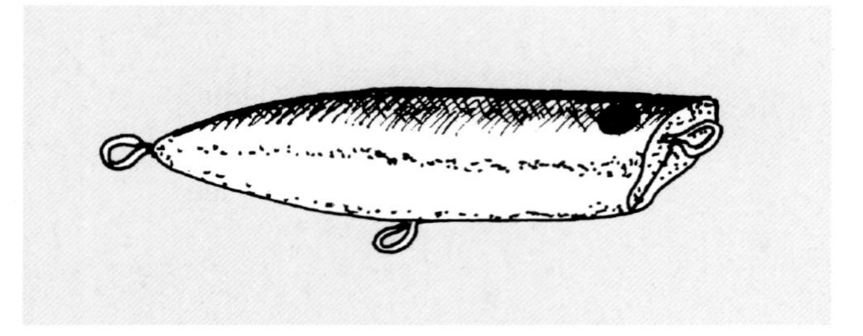

The core is sanded and painted.

11. Use water-based acrylic paint on the top of the core. Other types of paint will interact with the casting resin and are not appropriate. You can buy tubes of acrylic paint at any art counter. Spraying the paint on the core seems to give the best results. Black sequins make good eyes. They are glued in place. The cores can be varied slightly in size and density in order to make heavier lures or lures that float higher. Colors can also be varied. Using yellow as an undercoat and spraying blue over it produces a nice green, for example.

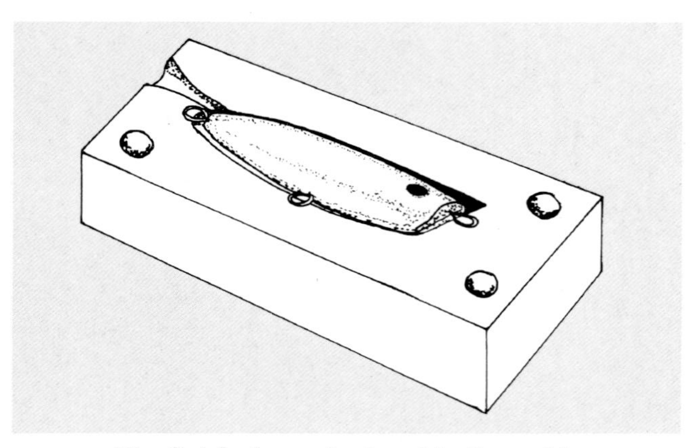

The finished core is placed in the mold.

12. When the paint is dry, the core is placed in the mold. The wire eyes of the core lie on the flat surface of the mold. Place the two pieces of the mold together and wrap wide rubber bands around the mold to keep it from leaking.

13. Mix clear plastic casting resin with some powdered fiberglass and a small amount of finishing resin plus catalyst. Stir this to the count of 100 and pour the resin into the mold. After 30 or 40 minutes, carefully take the mold apart. Cut the pouring tab away from the lure with a sharp knife. Allow the lure to harden for two days and then sand and polish where necessary.

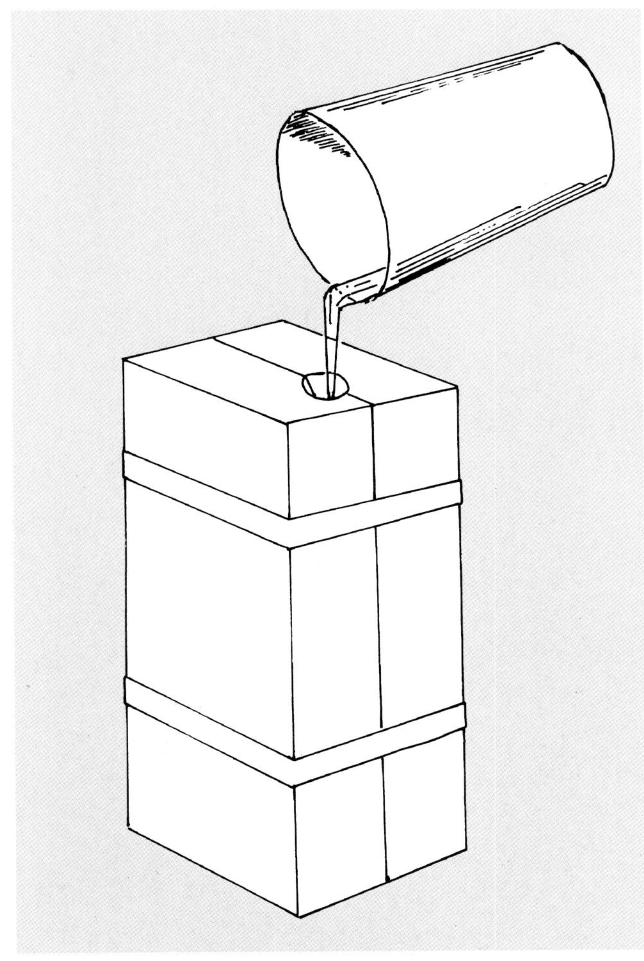

Resin is poured into the mold. Depending on the amount of catalyst used, the resin casting will take from 20 to 40 minutes to become stiff enough

14. Cut or bend treble hooks of the right size at the eye and slip them onto the lure's

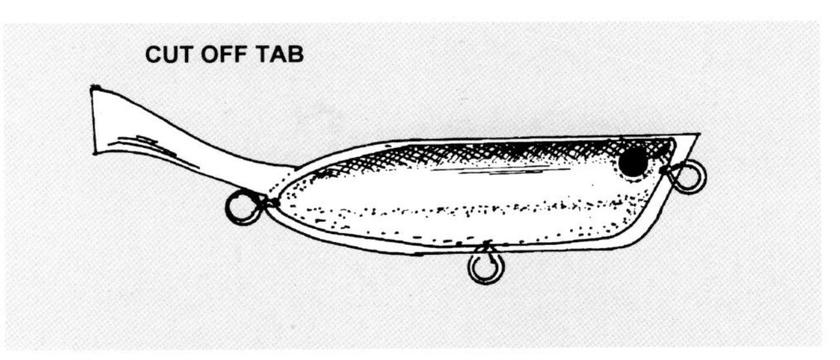

The pouring tab on the resin casting must be cut off and the lure is then sanded and polished. Finally hooks are bent onto the wire eyes.

eyeloops and rebend. The lure is finished! When the lure is made correctly, it rides on the surface at a slight angle, head up.

Test of a Super Lure

All last winter I worked on a new lure...a super lure designed to catch ulua in the 40- to 80-lb. range. The success of big stick lures such as pencil poppers and Molokai specials (a big stick lure) made me realize that the old adage "the bigger the lure the bigger the fish" contained a world of truth. A bigger lure can be seen more easily and can be cast farther. Like the original PILI, I made the new lure with an inner urethane core so that it would float and be stable. These super lures are big. They are seven and one-half inches long, over an inch in diameter, and weigh between 3 and 3½ oz. The front is scooped out and two number seven double strength treble hooks are used.

By late December I had carved several lures out of wood, put screw eyes in them and tried tthem out. One in particular had excellent action. I made a mold of this lure and began to make plastic lures with internal cores. Each time I made a lure I used more or less resin, painted the cores different colors, and tried them out in the marina behind my house. The action on the best lures was really excellent. I had Jeff Konn come over and practice with them and he tossed one, using a 12-ft. pole, over 90 yds.

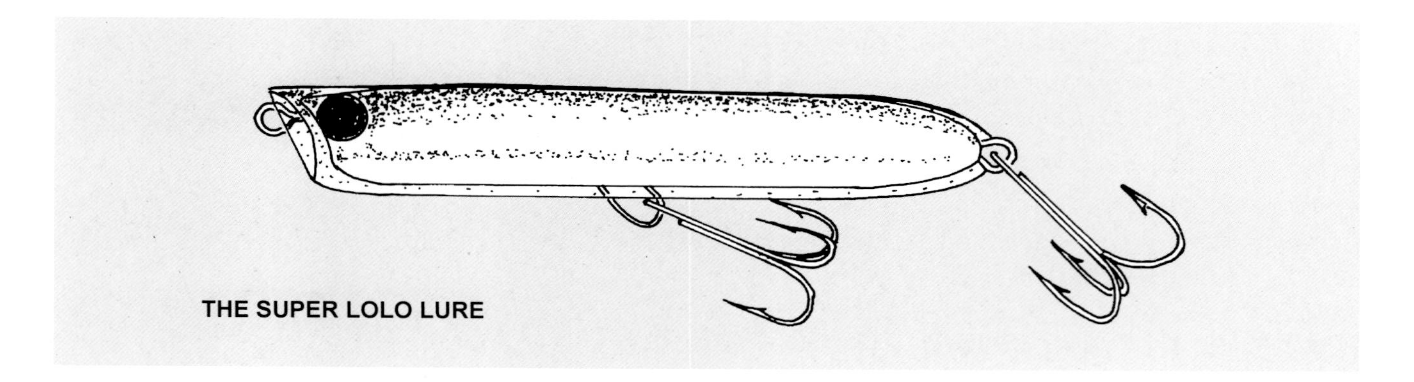

A line class world record caught on a super LOLO lure.

I gave quite a few of these lures to fishermen hoping they would report back on their success. Unfortunately, it was an unusual winter and there were very few days when wind wasn't blowing the tops off the waves. Few went fishing. Finally, Jeff Konn talked Stan Wright and me into a Kaho'olawe trip at the end of March. Jeff said the moon and tide were just right, meaning we would be fishing well before the full moon and that the tide had only a short rise and fall during the day. The wind blew all month but a trough in the weather occurred during the last week of March, and we prepared to do some real fishing at a place that had never disappointed us. I would have a chance to try out the super lures that so far had only demonstrated that they could cook up a fuss on the surface of the water behind my house.

The day was perfect for fishing. Kimmy Bryce had the No-Ka-Oi-IV ready at Ma'alaea Harbor on Maui and we headed for the north face of Kaho'olawe while the morning air was still crisp. Only a slight swell greeted us and near the island it disappeared. There was very little break on the beaches and Captain

Bryce was able to maneuver the 37-ft. Tollycraft at will and close to the reef. A slight breeze out of the Northeast aided our downwind casts and all of us anticipated great action.

During the morning, we made several hundred casts but nothing stirred the surface of the water behind our offerings. Jeff used Gibb's pencil poppers. Stan used the standard PILI and then switched to black touts and several other lures and back again. I kept throwing my big new lure at every promising rock, hole, or bay. At 10:00 A.M. we hadn't yet had a strike.

Everywhere we could see bright orange-yellow file fish floating on the surface. Stan even hooked one on a retrieve. Whales blew three hundred yards off shore. There was a high overcast but still no ulua (giant jack). I kept switching among the new lures, changing their colors. It was while I was watching the action of a dark blue lure with silver sides that I had the first strike. A three pound 'omilu had attacked a lure almost half its size. The first fish on the new lure was in the box! Shortly thereafter, Jeff caught a silver papio on a green-backed pencil popper and we thought we might have misread the tide; that now our time had come.

It wasn't until the early afternoon, however, that we had further action. In one of the beautiful coral coves on the north side of the island, I threw the same blue lure almost 60 yds. to some darker water behind a coral bank. Immediately the water exploded and the line started to zip from the reel. The fish dove behind the coral. There was little room to move the boat. Suddenly the line began running out at an alarming rate. I put slight tension on the line and came up empty. The coral had cut the 16-lb. line. The fish kept fighting the large plug and we saw it clearly, an 'omilu of about 12 lbs., cruising along the top of the reef.

After that experience, everyone went back to surface lures. Half an hour later, in another cove, another big bluefin trevally jumped a silver super lure and a real fight was on. I lightened my drag—you get a feeling for the way the drag should be by making a few pulls through the bail by hand. It is my opinion that fishermen horse too many fish. We are too anxious and we fight too close to the limits of the line. In this case, I was using 8-kg Trilene line. But the pole I use is over ten feet long, giving me great leverage even with a light drag.

The fish was deep but stayed in front of the bow of the boat. Its surges were controlled enough so that Kimmy could back out of the cove. After eight or ten minutes we could see color, a silvery blue, shimmering three fathoms below us. I gradually eased the fish to the surface. It was much bigger than I had anticipated. The mate, Jim Housh, came with a gaff and we had the fish on board. We weighed it on Stan's spring scale at 14½ lbs. Later at the Safeway store in Kahului, Maui, an electronic scale registered the weight at 14.41 lbs. Stan's spring scale was pretty accurate!

Shortly after I caught this record fish, Stan had a hit on an orange and black-striped PILI that looked much like the floating file fish. Another 'omilu fought back and forth across the ship's bow, an 11-pounder. Stan handled the fish well and the fish was netted on the side of the boat with little difficulty. Stan caught another 'omilu on the same lure and that was the end of the day's fishing.

We had caught five big fish. We had 11 strikes. I don't think I will ever know why there weren't more hits, but I believe the explosion of filefish had most predators satisfied. But I was also satisfied. I knew that the knew SUPER lure worked. It could catch small fish and big fish. I had caught a line class record. I had been with friends.

HOW TO CATCH THE BIG ONE

Knots and Connections

To capture the big fish, your gear must be in good order and you must know how to make the right connections. The following knots have proven to me to be the best. The angler should practice tying the knots so that they become simple and easy. That way you can tie them quickly under stress—for example, when the big ones are around and they have just ripped off your lure.

The Uni-knot: The best knot I have ever used is the Uni-knot developed by Vic Dunaway. I have lost hundreds of fish for one reason or another but only rarely has this knot failed. In the few cases of failure the knot was poorly tied. Usually not enough loops are taken. Use at least eight loops with the new **kevlar** lines. A nice thing about the Uni-knot is that, with a little practice, it can be tied very quickly.

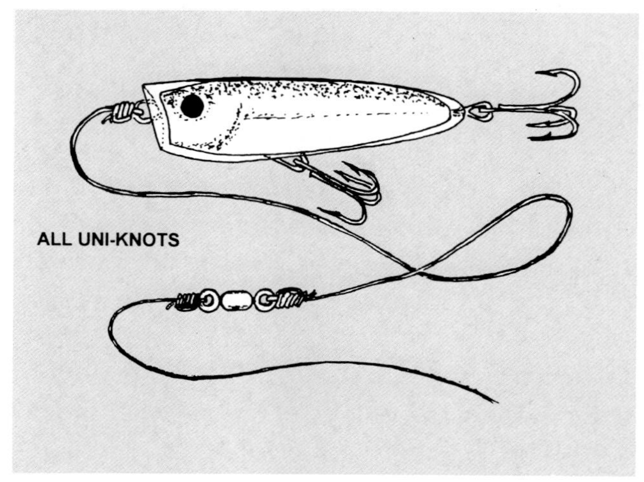

Vic Dunaway's Uni-knot can be used for almost every connection.

On the first pass through the eye of a swivel or lure hold the loop and the two lines with the left thumb and forefinger. The lighter the line the more passes you have to make. After each pass, I temporarily hold the end of the line in my mouth.

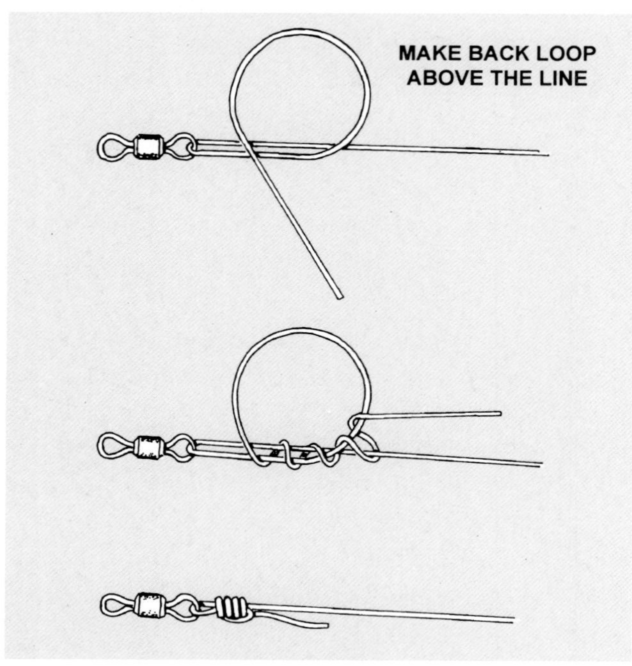

The Uni-knot is most easily tied by making a back loop above the line.

Leader to Line: One of the most difficult connection problems occurs when I want to tie a long, heavy leader to a light line. Take, for example, tying an 60-lb. test leader to an 8-lb. test main line. The longer the leader, the greater the likelihood that you will be able to land the big one. Sometimes I want to use the longest leader permitted by the International Game Fish Association (IGFA) which is up to 15 ft. long.

When you are ready to cast, even when using a long pole, the lure should be no more than 40 inches away from the rod tip. Otherwise, it is difficult or dangerous to handle the lure. What I sometimes like to do is to reel several feet of leader up into the guides. The leader is tied directly to the mainline with a knot small enough to pass easily through the eye of the tip during the cast.

The Bimini Twist: Years ago, after losing a giant ulua because I couldn't tie a good knot, I spent five hours tying and trying different knots. I had my best result using the double loop of a Bimini Twist and then tying two Uni-knots using the double loop and the leader. I tied this knot seven times and purposely pulled until the line broke. Seven times the line parted and left the knot intact!

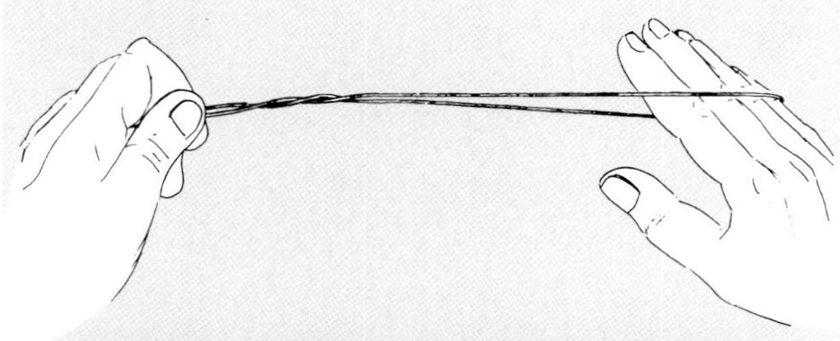

ROTATE LOOP END 15 TO 20 TIMES,TWISTING IT.

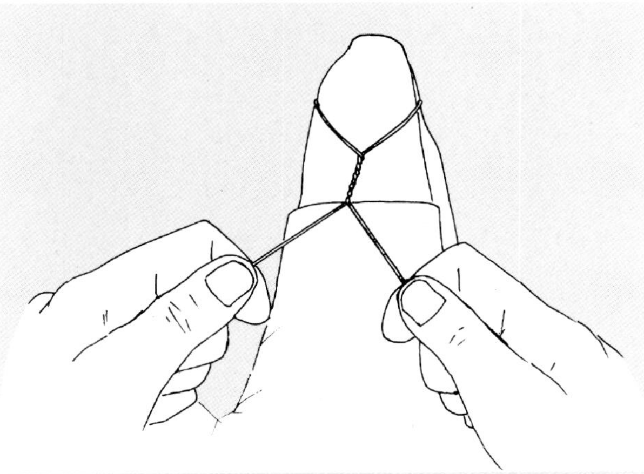

SPREAD LOOP AROUND YOUR KNEE. FORCE TWISTS TOGETHER BY PULLING TAG ENDS.

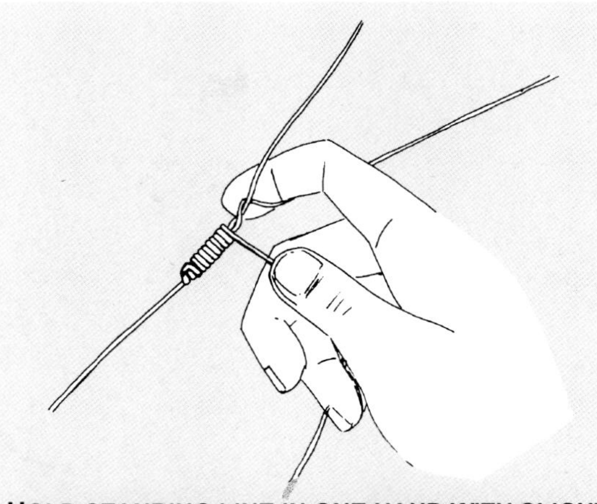

HOLD STANDING LINE IN ONE HAND WITH SLIGHT TENSION. WITH OTHER HAND MOVE TAG END AT RIGHT ANGLE TO TWISTS. TAG END WILL WANT TO ROLL OVER TWISTS. PLACE FOREFINGER IN THE CROTCH OF LOOP AND PULL FINGER TOWARD TWISTS LETTING TAG LINE

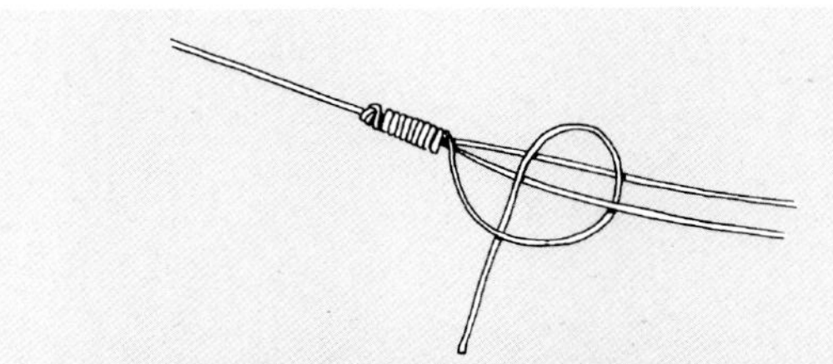

TAKE A HALF- HITCH AROUND NEAREST LEG OF THE LOOP AND PULL TIGHT.

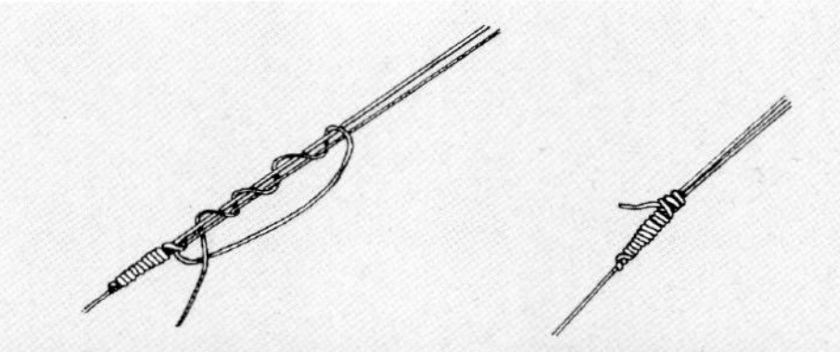

TAKE THREE MORE TURNS INSIDE ANOTHER HALF-HITCH AROUND BOTH LEGS OF LOOP .

The Bimini twist takes a little practice but after a while it get easier. The secret is to relax just enough tension as the forefinger pulls down on the twists.

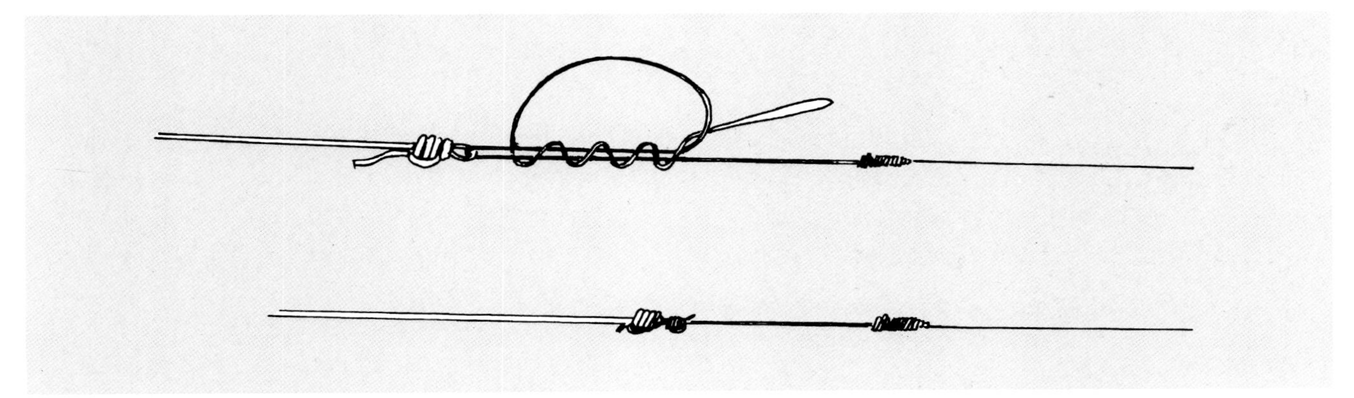

Tie the Bimini Twist in the main line. Tie a Uni-knot to create a small loop in the leader. Then tie the double line of the Bimini to the loop in the leader.

Wire: When trolling between spots and if wahoo, tanquique (the Pacific king mackerel) or barracuda are in the vicinity, I switch to short #6 or #7 stainless steel leaders. The key to using stainless steel leaders is that the initial wraps (after the leader has been passed through the eye of lure or swivel) must be "coat hanger" or "hay bail" twisted. That is, each wire must be twisted around the other before the short end is wrapped around the other. It is convenient to form a little crank with the short end and crank off the excess wire. My boyhood friend and commercial king fisherman has caught thousands of fish using this wrap.

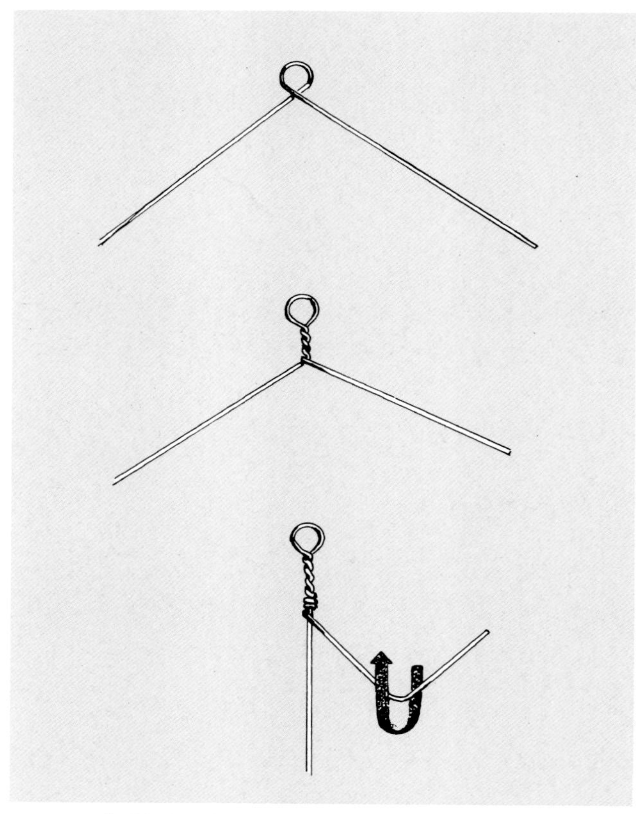

1. I initially bend the wire around a nail in order to create a loop.

2. Take at least five or six "hay bail" twists and then two or three straight wraps.

3. Bend the tail of the wire at 90 degrees.

4. Make the short end of the wire into a crank and twist it off in a clean break.

Coated Wire Cable: The only trouble with stainless wire is that it lacks flexibility. It is easily kinked and twisted and, when that happens, it has to be abandoned. The steel wire's lack of flexibility hampers the action of the lure and dramatically reduces the number of hits. One solution is to use plastic-coated cable. A popular brand is Sevalon. Sevalon is what the name implies--seven strands of wire encased in plastic.

If you use cable, secure it with lead sleeves that must be crimped. Insert a sleeve on the cable. Next, pass the cable through the eye of the lure and back through the sleeve. Crimp the sleeve with a pair of special pliers. Be sure to match the sleeves to the coated wire. It is more difficult to make up such a leader than it is to tie a regular nylon leader, but, if toothy barracuda are cutting you off, it may be worth the trouble.

I always take two or three such leaders already crimped to a lure, just in case. When crimping mono leaders, less crimping and more spread at the loop end of the sleeve reduces the chance of cutting the leader.

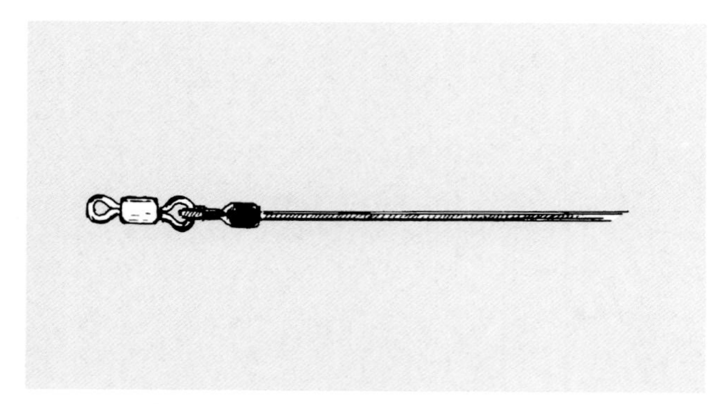

Coated wire cable is usually crimped with a lead sleeve. Slip the sleeve on the leader before

Swivels and Hooks

Swivels: It is not necessary to use a swivel if the lure swims upright and doesn't spin on the "retrieve" or when trolling. Few lures, however, are

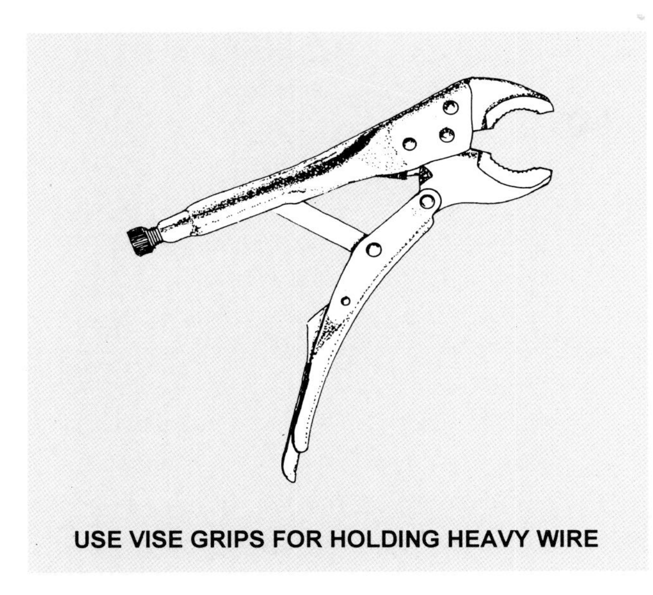

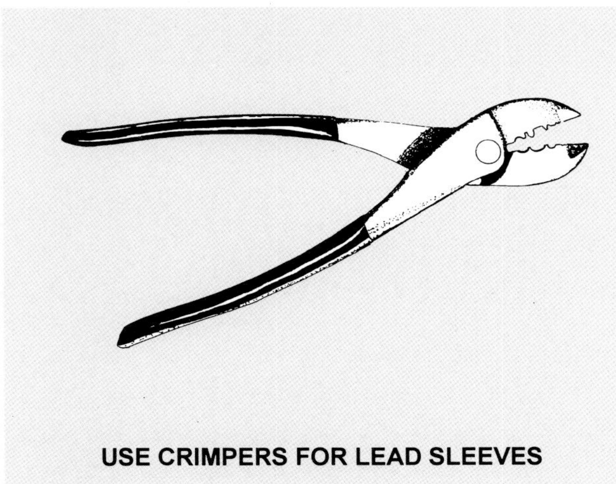

Use vise grip pliers to hold heavy wire when making hay-bail twists. Use crimpers for sleeves on cable.

so constituted, and in most cases it is important to use a swivel between the line and the leader. Simple barrel swivels work quite well. It is not necessary, however, to use a 200-lb. test swivel with 16-lb. test line. You do need a swivel large enough for the leader to pass through and also large enough so that it doesn't get jammed in the tip of the rod when bringing in the lure. Black swivels are less apt to be hit by small fish then shiny, stainless ones.

Use only one swivel: The fewer connections you make when tying your line to the lure, the better. The best case is to tie the line directly to the lure. This **(1)** improves the action of the lure, **(2)** makes the lure more realistic because there is no leader or swivel for the fish to see, and **(3)** ensures that there is only one connection that can break down.

Never use a clip swivel when spinning for big fish. This simply adds two more connections to the ones you have already made. Suppose you make: (1) a knot from line to swivel, (2) a knot from swivel to leader, (3) a knot from leader to clip-swivel, (4) a clip-swivel connection to lure and (5) connecting lure to hooks via rings. Further, suppose that each connection is 95 percent sure. The total rig, however, is only as secure as the product of the probabilities, or 77 percent (i.e. 95 x .95 x .95 x .95 x .95 = .77).

When fishing for the big ones in the rough coral, you will need a leader, so this means at least two (90 percent) or three (85 percent) connections. Eliminate the rings that most lures come with and attach the hooks directly to the hook eyes.

Hooks: I like to use #2, #3, #4 and #7 double-strength Mustad treble hooks on the lures that I make. I often replace the hooks on purchased lures because **(1)** they are not strong enough or **(2)** they are tied to the lure with split rings, which are usually not soldered and are therefore a weak link.

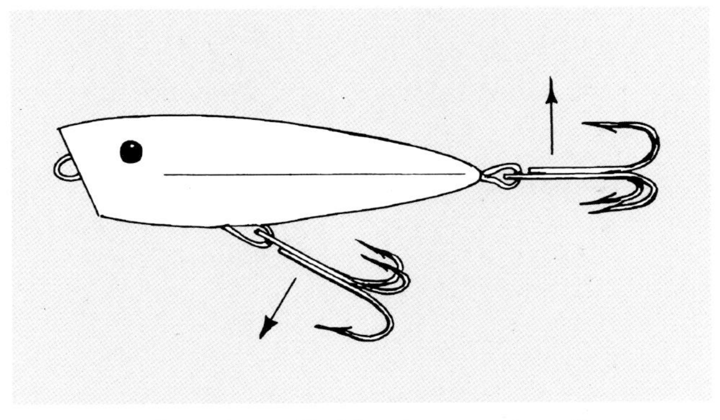

Place the welded hook up on the tail and down at the belly.

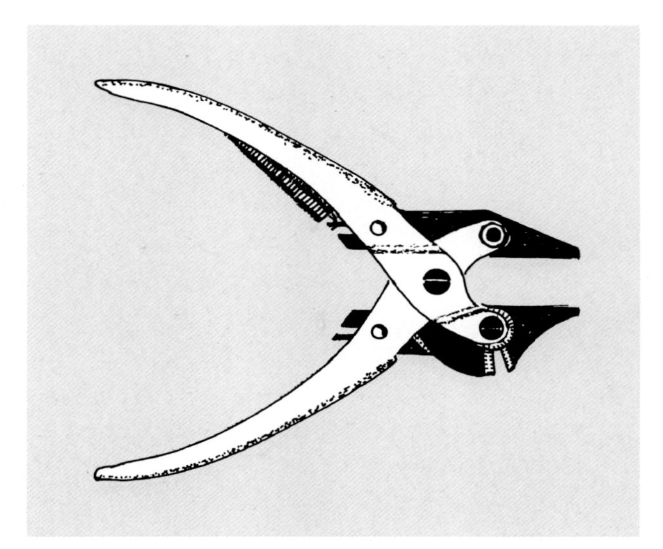

The topwater fisherman needs a pair of English electrician's pliers. The compound cutter is very strong.

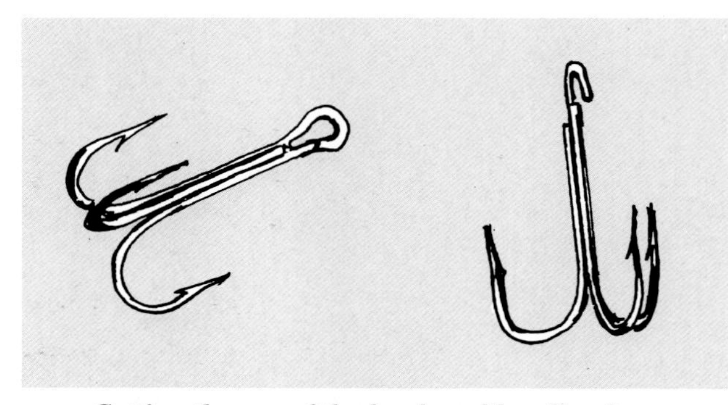

Cutting the eye of the hook and bending it on for the strongest connection.

When placing treble hooks on a lure, take note of the one hook that has been welded to the other two. This noncontinuous hook should always point up when it is placed at the end of a lure and point down when it is placed on the bottom of the lure.

To cut tough hooks, you will need a pair of English electrician's pliers. The pliers are good for all kinds of things, but they have a sharp compound cutter that is just right for cutting through the eye of a hook. The cut is made just above the point where the eye meets the shaft. The eye is bent out, the hook is placed, and the eye is bent back into position. It is also possible to purchase treble hooks that have been precut. These keep the hooks better because the cut has been galvanized.

Cutting and bending hooks to a lure is simple and makes the strongest connection between the lure and the hooks. When I travel, I put lures and hooks in separate boxes. When I'm ready to fish, I pull two hooks from their box and bend them onto the lure. This takes less than a minute. The alternative, which is to transport lures with hooks already attached, can be a nightmare. Lures and hooks together can be as difficult to take apart as a Chinese puzzle.

Fishing Tip: I store all the hooks in a small container where they will get tangled up. It is a simple matter, however, to untangle them. Place the cluster of hooks in a larger box or tray and bounce this tray up and down several times. The hooks come apart like magic.

If you use line heavier than 16-lb. test, you may wish to graduate to #4, #5 or #6 treble hooks. One time I got the largest Daiwa reel I could find, a 9000, and I used 50-lb. test line and an 11-ft. surf pole. I put #4 treble hooks on a big lure. I cast this rig as far as I could at the North Point of Christmas Island. When a big ulua hit, I cranked the drag down tight. A few brief bursts of line came off the reel and then nothing. I pulled in the lure, and two of the rear hooks had been pulled straight open. The hooks were too small for the line.

In general, I have found that the hooks should be stronger than the line. This allows you to grab the leader with some confidence when a big fish is close. Remember, however, that few hooks can handle the dead weight of a large fish. Probably more hooked fish are lost at the boat than in any other specific area. Most fisherman are just too anxious. A green fish can be a nightmare to handle, whereas a fish that comes to the surface and

This dolphin was caught on light line and light hooks.

lays on its side can be taken like a baby. What this means is that all fisherman should take more time fighting and playing the fish.

One time a large dolphin (fish) hit a small trolled lure. The lure had small #1/0 trebles and the line was 16-lb. test. Several times the fish came to the boat close enough for us to see that the hooks were only tenderly placed on the outside of the mouth. By taking time we were able to save this fish and have sauteed mahi'mahi for supper.

I most often use #3/0 double-strength hooks because the strong jaws of a big trevally will crush the #2/0 Mustads and make them look like pretzels. I have tried using double stainless hooks with little success. These hooks don't seem to swing right on a lure. They also are difficult to keep sharp. In Pohnpei, I tried lures with simple stainless double hooks in them and lost fish after fish. They would hit but fail to get hooked. It can't be stressed enough that you should keep your hooks sharp. Check to see if the tip of the hook will catch on your thumbnail. If not, it needs to be sharpened. The larger the hook, the sharper it needs to be.

Lure Color and Action

An island fisherman, Vernon Isono, showed me a PILI casting lure that he brought back from Christmas Island. It had a light-blue back with lime-green striping.

"This was the only lure that would catch papio (small jack) at the Korean Wreck," Vernon said,. "This lure caught 18 fish. Can you make me another?"

I made Vernon several more striped lures and he caught fish with these as well. I was never one for using striped lures. Now I know better.

I had always used light-green and white lures for island fishing. Jeff Konn, an expert fisherman, swears by dark-green and white. Wayne Okubo, veteran island fisherman, was always after me to make pink lures for use off the Big Island of Hawai'i. Wayne tells me that some fisherman want blue and blue-striped lures for casting around the buoy off Hilo. Rick Kamita, former proprietor of Fuji's Tackle store, likes a silver and white-striped lure for fishing off the reef runway.

How important is color? Will any lure with good action work? One day, when the sky was dark and the sea was flat, Mike Sakamoto, of TV's "Fishing Tales," was tossing a giant "Moloka'i Special," using a short stiff, rod and a conventional reel. The "special" was a tapered piece of wood painted black on top and yellow underneath. Mike retrieved this lure at a furious pace, making the lure stand on its tail, wagging back and forth. It looked like a spooked needlefish. Mike quickly caught an 'omilu weighing around 6 lbs. On his next cast, a giant ulua jumped on his lure. After a brief tussle, both fish and lure were gone.

That same day, Jeff Konn caught a blue jack with a blue-blacked Rebel Windcheater and Photographer Stan Wright caught three fish using a dark-gray PILI. When Stan had a big fish strip all the line off his spinning reel, I started to pay attention. I had insisted on using my "tried and true" light-green lure, but had come up empty. When Mike, using another black-and-white piece of broomstick, hauled in another 6 pounder, I changed my lure to a dark-blue solid with silver stripes.

I spun this dark winking lure out toward the western horizon just outside the rocks of the bay in which we were drifting. The skipper hollered from the upper deck as the water parted behind the lure and a fish in the world-record class streamed the 16-lb. test line from the Penn 550SS. After 17 minutes, the line came up slack and broken. I immediately went to my fishbox and looked for every dark-blue, black or gray lure. I came up with a dark-purple and gray-backed lure.

A short time later in the same bay, I was rewarded with the fight of a lifetime, when a 33-lb. ulua chased this lure across the shadowy sand, giving everyone a view of the savage hit right in front of the bow of the boat. Fortunately the big trevally stayed on top, and we were able to back him into deeper water. After 30 minutes of careful tug-of-war Mike was able to gaff the fish at the swimstep.

A 33-lb. ulua caught on 16-lb. test line. Doubling is a great experience

That trip pretty well convinced me that the old saying, "Dark day, dark lure" reflects a world of truth. But why should this be so? Wouldn't a lighter lure be easier to see on a dark day? I've thought about what it takes to be successful and I think the answer lies in the following basics.

1. Use a natural-looking bait. The MULI, Rapala, and PILI lures are natural looking lures. On at least six occasions I have seen these lures struck while they were floating motionless and unattended. Color is one way of achieving naturalness. I believe that the color of a lure should generally match a bird's-eye view of the color of the water's surface. Bait fish follow this evolutionary scheme, and lures should also. I'm convinced that is the reason why dark lures were so successful on the overcast day at Kaho'olawe. They looked more natural. Lime green and blue are the colors of the reef fish, such as wrasse, that dominate the waters off the Korean Wreck on the southern shore of Christmas Island. Blue, blue-black and purple are deep-water colors and the color of flying fish. Silver and white match the color of lizard fish in the sand off Hickam Field, Hawai'i. Green is great in shallow water or over reefs when the sun is shining bright.

Scientists who study trevally indicate that the giant trevally (*C. ignoblis*) and bluefin trevally (*C. Melampygus*) are the most prolific trevally in the Pacific. These fish are great predators, and their diet consists primarily of other reef fish. Most often eaten are the colorful small wrasse, parrotfish and goatfish.

Next are big-eyed scads, damsel fish, squirrel fish, surgeon fish, file and trunkfish. The giant trevally differs from the bluefin trevally in that it eats many more eels and large crustaceans, such as lobster and crab. While many of the reef prey are quite colorful, some, like many surgeon fish, are almost black.

The fisherman, therefore, needs to try a variety of colors on the reef to see which bait fish is most plentiful in a particular area. My fishing companion, Richard Murakami, told me that he was fishing a particular reef in Pohnpei and that black lures caught fish at a rate of three-to-one for other colors of lures. Some reef fish also have big eyes and many butterfly fish have "big eye" protective coloration on their tails and bodies. This suggests that some lures that you carry should have big eyes emulating squirrel fish and scad.

Explaining the early morning success of a "passionate pink" lure is more difficult. While mempachi (red sqirrelfish) is one favorite food of ulua, the "glow-pink" is not truly approximated in nature. It has been shown that surface feeders, like mahi'mahi, can see different colors clearly. The colors that fish see, however, are changed because

The MULI is made to look like a flying fish or mullet. The PILI is the size and shape of a sardine.

the density of the water acts as a filter. Red and orange, with long wave lengths, will show the greatest change due to absorption. In the early morning or during a rain, the pink lures will be a shade of gray but they will be easily seen. I have rarely caught fish in the bright sun using these colorful lures, but they are effective at other times. It is well known that the pelagic fish, tuna for example, see only shades of blue. But they are attracted to blue and pink lures. In this case, the pink must serve as an effective contrast.

I took black "Creek Chub" lures to the sand flats of Christmas Island and never had a hit. It didn't occur to me then, but there aren't any black bait fish inside the lagoon. On the way home from a trip to Kaho'olawe, however, we caught one fish after another on small black-tailed jigs by flipping them up against the rocks just like the jumping jacks that they resembled. I didn't realized it at the time, but the dark-green lures that I made resembled the coloration of many Hinalea (wrasse), a favorite food of the bluefin trevally. One can conclude that color is important and should match the predominate prey.

I also believe, but have less support for the idea, that fish get conditioned to the local food source. If, for example, the o'ama (baby goatfish) have been running, then a lure that resembles the shape, color and action of, say, a squirrel fish (mempachi) will be less effective than a lure that contains the pink, yellow, white, or gray seen in o'ama.

2. Use an **active lure**. The success of topwater lures is based on the action that they generate. The lack of explosive quality is one reason swimming lures are not as productive as poppers. The built-in action of the Rapala is great for trolling but isn't dynamic enough to consistently attract a reef predator like the ulua.

The rougher the water the more action is needed to attract attention. Action, however, is not by itself enough. I once made a perfectly clear popping lure with just two black eyes showing. Jeff tried this lure at Christmas Island and he told me that the action caused the pursuit of a few fish but there were no strikes. The fish has to see something!

Casting and Fighting

Learn to place and maneuver the lure. Rick Kamita told me that some fishermen were using the same lure that he was and couldn't "buy" a strike while he was pulling in one fish after another. Rick's pole was a 10-foot graphite, and he could cast 10 to 20 yards farther than his partners. He was reaching the edge of the reef from the boat outside, and the others were falling short.

As long as I have been fishing, I feel that only about one out of five of my casts is a really good one. Placement is a kind of art. If you are fishing from the outside, next to cliffs, you can't approach too closely because the boat can scare the fish. The lure, however, must land within 3 feet of the white water. This is because the trevally are lying in the shadows of the reef, which is growing at the base of the cliffs. They either do not see the lure or will not venture far from this familiar territory.

When throwing from the reef, one has to think about where the backwash of the wave runoff occurs. Outside these awas, or runoff channels, the predators will be waiting. When spinning from a boat, it is important sometimes to be able to toss the lure right up onto the shallow water of the reef and drag it back to you like a fish darting to deeper water. A careful watch is made so that the lure can run down the coral fingers that project out into the sea. If the bottom is over 50 feet deep and there is no sign of coral, then there is less chance that a reef predator will come to the surface. Foraging ulua are sometimes caught away from the reef, but few other reef predators are.

When spinning against the wind, the cast should start slowly, with bent knees, and end explosively. A low overhead cast is most effective.

Most lures will not create enough fish-like activity by themselves. Today's lures come in a variety of shapes and sizes, and each one has characteristics that can be exploited by the type of cast and retrieve that you make. The length of the pole determines the line of attack that the line

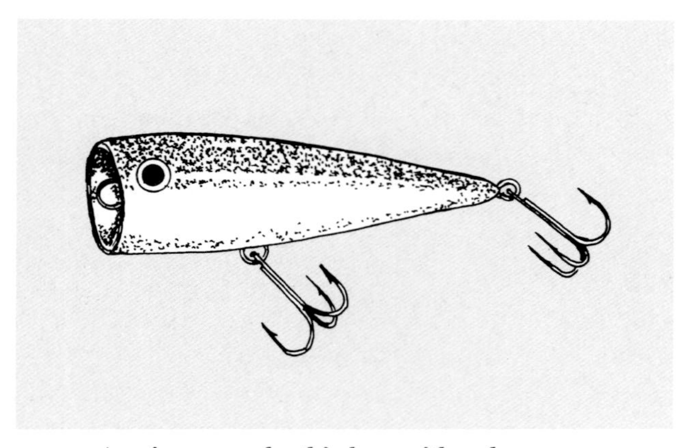

Aussies swear by this lure with a deep cup.

makes with the lure's head. If the rod is held too high during the retrieve, it can pull the head of the lure completely out of the water and reduce the popping action. When fishing from a cliff, this problem is exaggerated, and heavy lures with deep cups in front may have to be used.

The most successful surface poppers in Australia are black and have deep, concave cups on the front. They are difficult to bring in, but work well from cliffs.

When fishing the flats or walking a reef, the rod can be lowered in order to impart a different action or submerge a lure. The speed of the retrieve should also match the type of lure. Mike Sakamoto's stick lures were so successful I tried to pull in a PILI lure that fast. Even though I had a 5-to-1 reel ratio, I couldn't keep up. More importantly, I was taking some action off the lure. Meanwhile, Stan Wright, with greater tip action and slower speed, was getting more hits than anyone.

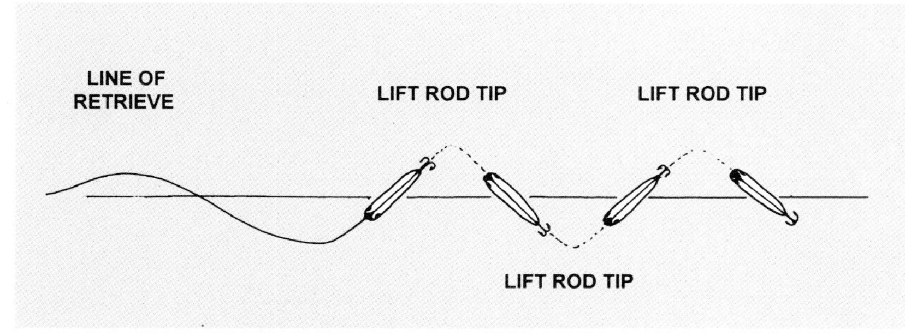

Good anglers learn to move the lure back and forth across the line of retrieve.

Dick Cushman, an international fisherman, told me that he had carefully watched the difference between the quicker bluefin trevally and the bigger ulua's reaction to a surface popper. A faster retrieve would excite the smaller fish and they would beat the big ulua to the lure. When the retrieve was slowed down, then the big ones would come up, almost slowly, and gulp the bait. Dick used this method to catch a 93 lb. ulua!

I like to "walk the dog" when pulling in a popper. That is, I lift the rod tip and turn the reel crank at the same time, then pause while lowering the tip, and repeat this motion. This causes a darting action back and forth across the line of pull. I vary this basic pattern by the amount and direction that I lift the rod. I also vary the length of the pause.

I find it helpful to find some quiet water and practice different speeds and motions. Even a beginner can tell if the action he is getting is fish-like. After a while you get a feel for the right action. Sometimes when the placement is perfect and the feel is right, you can call your shots. On those occasions, I am almost alway rewarded with big hits. If you use a popping lure, try to have it pop or push water as it dances back and forth. Sometimes long, straight pulls with a definite pause will draw strikes.

Fish slackwater and a rising tide. Large reef fish instinctively move to deeper water on an outgoing tide, because it is dangerous for active reef predators to get caught in tide pools while the tide is going out. One calm day, my son Derek and I caught two 23-pound trevally inside the north reef at Christmas Island in 4 feet of water. The tide had changed to come in an hour before. Earlier, on an outgoing tide, we had traversed a mile of reef without seeing a big fish. Here, the right tide and the flat coral bottom permitted the opportunity to land the big one.

If you have a choice, it is better to take advantage of the terrain. When fishing inside a shallow lagoon, throw to the edge of the reef, rather than over it. When on the reef's edge, throw well over the wave break. Fish the edges of the coral, rather than the top.

Fish with the rod, not the reel. Once you have a fish on, try to hold it in position. This tires a fish even though there doesn't seem to be much strain. The advantage of holding high with big fish is that they don't make sudden line-breaking moves. Once the fish gives ground, steadily pull the rod tip toward you and reel quickly as you tip the rod down to pick up more line. When using spinning gear, you should rarely crank the reel when there is a strain on the line. The reel is used primarily for picking up the line that the rod makes available.

When pulling a fish up from deep water, pull as slowly as possible to prevent line from coming off the spool. It is always rewarding to catch a big fish on light line. Whether it is a 16-lb. 'omilu on 8-lb. test line or a 33-lb. ulua on 16-lb. test line, "doubling up" is an achievement.

How Much Drag?

Of all the errors I have made fishing over the years, the most serious has been to have set too tight a drag. A good experiment is to rig up your line, reel and pole. Tie a spring scale, firmly, to some low spot. Next tie your line to the hook end of the scale, and check your drag. I like to set my drag at around 25 percent of the breaking strength of the line. I have a partner check the scale to see at what weight the drag releases the line. It is truly surprising how hard you can pull your long pole against 8-lb. test line with the drag set at 25 percent of the line's breaking strength. You can always loosen the drag when fishing, but rarely should you tighten down on a spool. An exception would be when a big fish is "spooling your reel," that is, taking all the line. Then you may have to do something.

Telling the Tide

When I was a young teacher in Sarasota, Florida, I used to set gill nets for mullet with Mr. Drumwright. We would go out at night, and "Drummy" would wait for the tide to change. "We'll wait for low tide when the mullet will be coming out of the woods (the mangroves)," he said. He would look at the moon and tell me whether the tide was "right" or not. One night when things were "right," we netted over 4000 lbs. of mullet and sold them for a nickel a pound.

The moon rises at sunset off Vaisala Beach, Savai'i.

Every reef fisherman wants to fish a rising tide. A high, rising tide allows finny predators an opportunity to actively invade the reef and search for food. The local fishermen that I know are always planning their fishing to coincide with the "right" tide. This usually means they would like a change of tide in the morning and a rising tide for most of the day; say, from 7:00 in the morning until 1:00 or 2:00 in the afternoon. Unfortunately, a high, rising tide is rare in the morning in the Pacific, but some secondary or smaller high tides do occur.

Fishermen who fish at night like a full moon. They say that the fish can see the bait better. On the other hand, daytime veterans tell me that they like to go fishing 6 to 8 days before the full moon. In a recent article, however, the International Game Fish Association suggests that fish catches are unaffected by the moon's phases. Nevertheless, the tides do affect when and where you are able to go fishing.

In some areas, Hawai'i for example, tide charts are readily available. *Hawaii Fishing News* has a tide chart in each monthly issue and each year prints a *Moon and Tide Almanac*. But what if a chart isn't available or you want to fish away from charted waters? Many of the exotic places to fish in the Pacific lack tide charts. It is difficult to tell what is going to happen in places like Yap or Fiji, for example. One fall, in Pohnpei, we had to work harder for the fish we caught because we chose a week when the tide hardly rose at all.

How can we look at the moon and get an idea of when the tide will be right? When we look

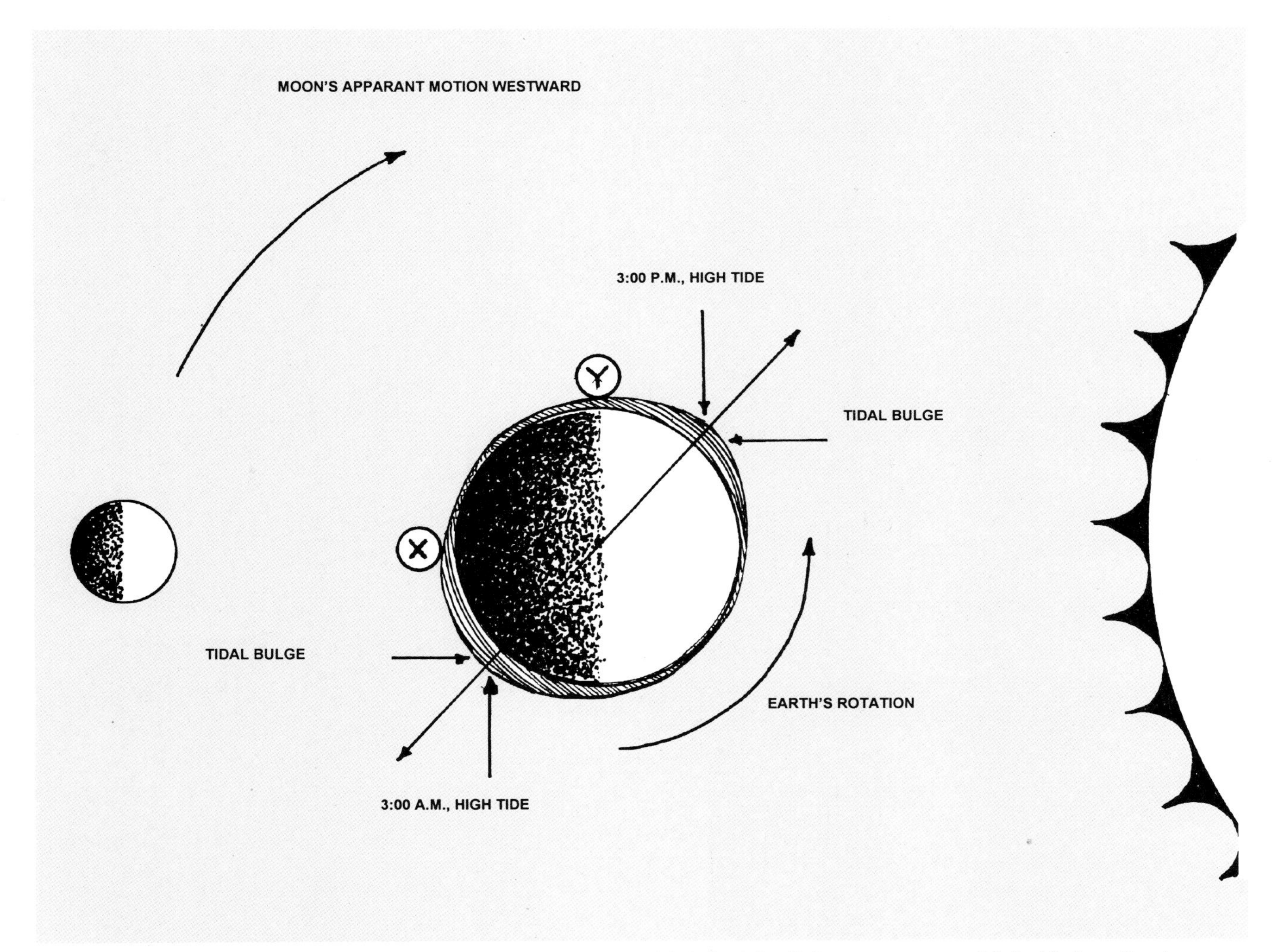

An observer at X sees the full moon directly overhead at midnight. The fisherman expects high tide in a few hours. The observer at Y sees the full moon rise at sunset. One high tide has occurred three hours earlier, and the next high tide will occur nine hours later at around 3:00 A.M. The apparent motion of the tidal bulge is that it follows the moon, but in reality the earth's rotation throws the tidal bulge ahead of the moon's gravitational pull.

up at the night sky (north of the equator) and see the moon, it is in one of its phases. That is, it is waxing

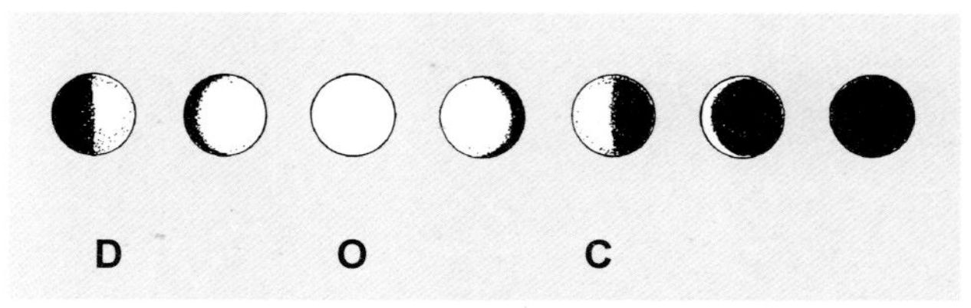

The nmenonic "What's up* DOC *?" tells the direction of the moon's phases.

(moving to full) or waning (moving to a new moon). You can tell which way the moon is going by recalling the mnemonic, "What's up **DOC** ?"

D O C - represents the direction of the moon's phases. The smooth curve of the letters **D** and **C** represent the lighted right and left edges or halves of the moon. The moon waxes, or gets brighter, when the smooth-curved edge of the moon is on the right, as in the letter **D**. If, on the other hand, you look up in the sky and see a smooth curve or crescent on the left, you know that the moon is waning. The **O** represents the full moon, and the blank space after the **C** represents the new moon. Just remember,"What's up **D-O-C- ."** If, however, you are located south of the equator you will have to reverse the order to **"C-O-D ."**

The moon's phases are determined by how much sunshine we are able to see reflected off the moon's surface. If the moon is between the viewer and the sun, it cannot be seen at all (a new moon) because no sunlight is reflected. When the moon rises at sunset, it is invariably a full moon because the sun is on the western horizon and the moon is on the opposite or eastern horizon. When you see half of a moon (first or third quarter phase), then the moon and sun are at right angles to the earth.

The moon and sun's gravity both pull on the earth. Of these two bodies, the moon has the greater influence on the fluid surface of the earth, about twice that of the sun. Gravity has the effect of pulling the surface of the sea in the general direction of the moon. But gravity squeezes the seas of the earth much like we might press on the sides of a round balloon. This causes the tide, like the balloon, to rise or bulge in opposite directions on the earth, that is, both toward and away from the moon.

It is convenient to think of the earth as stationary, with the moon and tide pattern moving rapidly west. At least that is the way it looks to us. In the illustration if you are the viewer at X and the full moon is directly overhead, it will be close to midnight. In the Pacific the high tide won't come for another three or four hours. If, however, you are a viewer at Y, then the full moon will be rising at sunset and it will be approximately another nine hours before high tide or around 3:00 the next morning. Actually the tidal bulge is "dragged" east ahead of the moon by the earth's rotation. The water "sticks" to the earth as it rotates. When a full moon rises at sunset, the high tide will already have occurred around 3:00 P.M. that afternoon.

When the sun and moon are on opposite sides of the earth (the full moon **O**) or when they are on the same side of the earth (the new moon ●), they are in line and the highest difference in high and low tides occur. The time when the high tides occur is also more consistent. For full and new

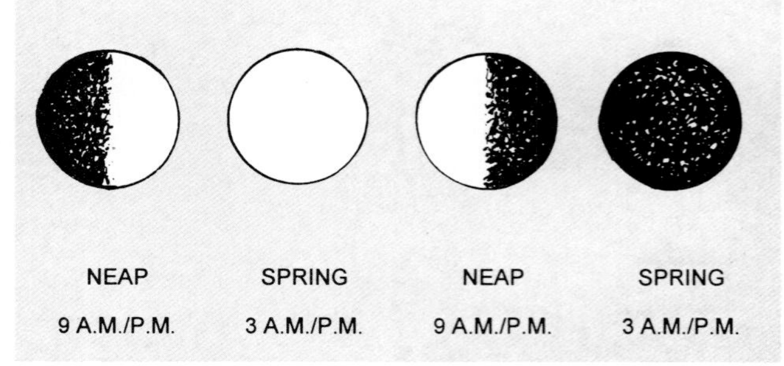

moons a high tide will occur around 3:00 a.m. and 9:00 p.m. in Hawai'i.

In the mid-Pacific islands there are two high and two low tides in a 24-hour period. The moon rises about 50 minutes later each day. This is

Fishing tip: Say the tide and the fishing were good on a particular day. In general, the same tide will occur about 50 minutes later the next day. You can plan to get up and go fishing an hour later. Because the tides rotate on two-week cycles, if the fishing proved good on a particular day and on a particular tide, it might be worthwhile to try again in two weeks, same time, same place. If, however, a good fishing tide is high at 3:00, then one week later it will be exactly opposite or low tide at that time.

because the moon is actually moving eastward on a longer 29-day revolution around the earth (the lunar month as opposed to a 28-day or four-week month based on the earth's rotation).

The next time you are away from a local tide chart remember that a high tide will already have occurred approximately three hours ahead of the rising moon. It will, therefore be about 9 more hours until a high tide occurs again. If the moon rises at sunset, a high tide will have already occurred that afternoon around 3:00. This will be the spring tide, or highest tide (spring comes from the Old English word springe, meaning "to swell").

When the moon is in its first or third quarter, it rises much later, around 11:00 or 12:00, and the high tide will vary from 7:30 to 9:30 morning and evening. Tides will be minimal, or neap tides (neap comes from the Old English nep, which means "scanty"). For the days in between, judge by adding a little less than an hour per day.

If the moon is starting to wane, you might still be up and able to observe the time of its rising. Say you observe the moon rise at 10:00 p.m. Then you are pretty sure that a high tide occurred 3 hours earlier at around 7:00 p.m. and another high will occur around 6:00 or 7:00 the next morning.

The times presented here are approximate, and should be used in a general way. They could be off by as much as two hours. This time frame should work similarly throughout the Pacific; that is, if you are on Guam and you see a full moon you can expect the next tide to be high around 3:00 a.m.

Professor Edwin Stroup, an oceanographer at the University of Hawai'i, kindly points out that this scheme may not work in some parts of the Pacific. In Tahiti, for example, the tide occurs at the same time each day, every day, no matter what the moon is doing. In other words, it is a solar tide.

The tide and moon depicted here works for Hawai'i and the Pacific. But on the East Coast of the United States you will have to establish the time of the high tides for each particular area and act accordingly.

Sometimes the water is flat and you can fish anywhere outside the edge of the reef

FISH YOU CAN CATCH

It would be difficult to describe all the fish that are possible to catch on the reef, but those predators that I have personally met, and that will crash a surface popper, are described in some detail.

In many cases, all tackle records for these fish have not been recorded or can be broken by the enterprising angler. In such cases the scientific names for genus and species are provided (See **A World Record for Any Angler**, p. 73).

Sometimes it is hard to detect the difference between one fish and another. With the IGFA's recognition of all tackle records for all game fish, proper classification becomes important.

Trevallys

Trevallys of the Pacific are among the strongest fighters pound for pound of any fish in the world. There are over ten different species of big jacks that will hit a surface lure. The giant trevally strikes with the ferocity of a tiger and pulls with the strength of a bull.

Most of the trevallys in the Pacific can qualify for all tackle records but you have to know which is which. On a trip to Pohnpei, in the shadow of the ancient ruins of Nan Madol, I caught a dusky

The same species (*C. ignoblis*) can have different color phases. The author on the left with a 40-lb. trevally caught off the north coast of Fanning Island and Chris Watanabe and Peter Arthur with a 35-lb. fish in Matalanim Harbor, Pohnpei.

black trevally. I thought that this was the true Black Trevally, (*Caranx lugubris*). Even its eyes were black. Later that afternoon, however, Chris Watanabe caught a 35-lb. silvery white trevally with identical markings.

Both of these fish had the same steep profile at the head and a deep body that marks the giant trevally (*C. ignoblis*). Only the color was different. The fact that the same species could take on such widely different coloration was amazing. Since then, I have caught several ulua with this dark coloring and must conclude that these fish were probably hiding under a ledge and had changed color to match their surroundings. Such color changes are just as remarkable for other trevally.

The trevallys head the list of the Pacific reef fighters. The jacks are without a doubt the toughest and most prolific gamefish on the reef. But how can we tell the different trevallys apart? How are they named and classified? First, all fish are in the class Pisces (fish). Under the class is the family *Carangidae* (pronounced ka-ran-guh-dee). One unique characteristic of the family *Carangidae* is that located just in front of the anal fin are two spines. Apparently all jack, pompano, rainbow runner, amberjack, and trevally have this unique characteristic.

Under the family, scientific names come in two parts: genus and species. The **genus** defines a number of animals with some common characteristics. Giant trevally and bluefin trevally are members of the **genus** *Caranx*. *Caranx* members are distinguished by two rows of small and large conical teeth in the upper jaw and a single, moderately sized row of teeth in the lower jaw. Finally, there is the **species** or unique group. **Species** are special in that they can breed only among themselves. The giant trevally, the common ulua, is the species *ignoblis*, while the bluefin is the species *melampygus*.

Identifying Trevallys

It is pretty easy to tell the **bluefin** trevally from the **giant** trevally because the bluefin has a more pointed face and usually shows bright blue fins. The real difference, however, is that the bluefin has a breast that is completely scaled, whereas *C. ignoblis* has a breast that has only a small patch of scales. Another difference is the placement of the eye. In C. ignoblis the eye is inside a vertical line ddrawn from the end of the jaw and in *C. melampygus* the eye lies outside the jaw

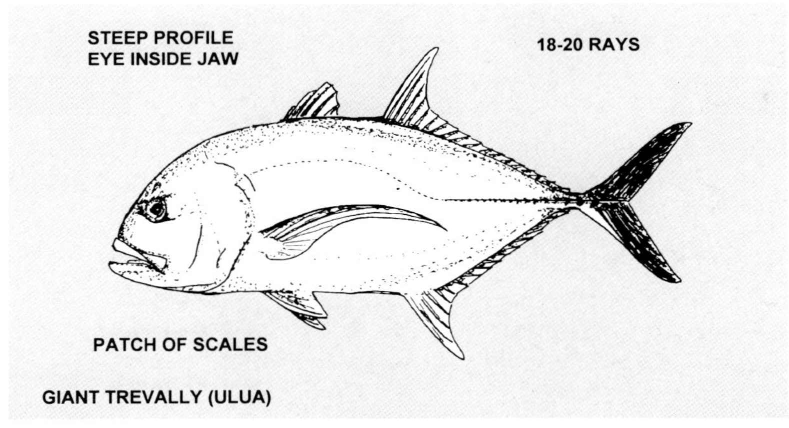

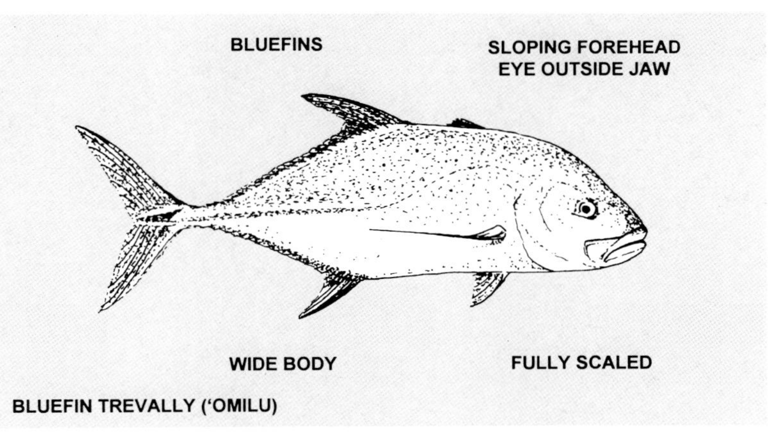

This figure shows the difference between the bluefin and giant trevally. Notice the placement of the eye relative to the mouth.

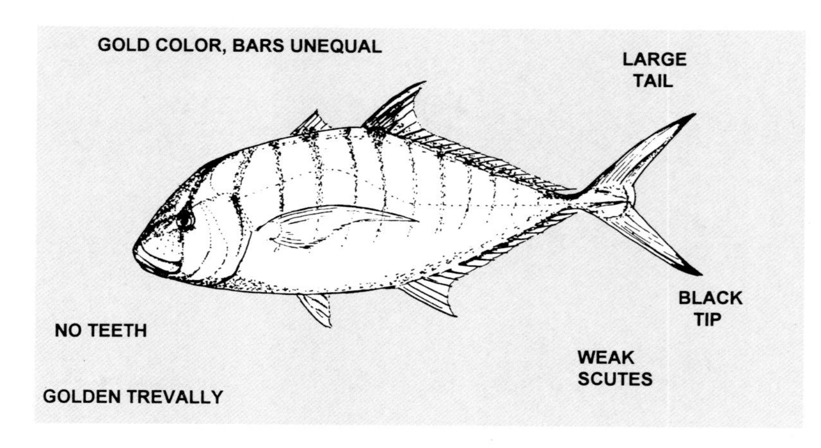

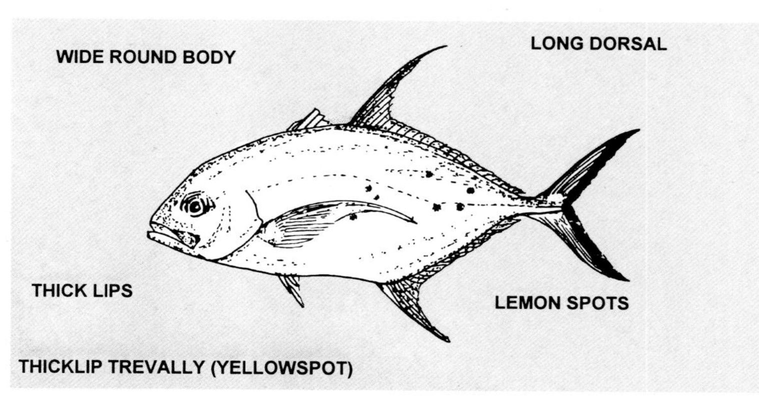

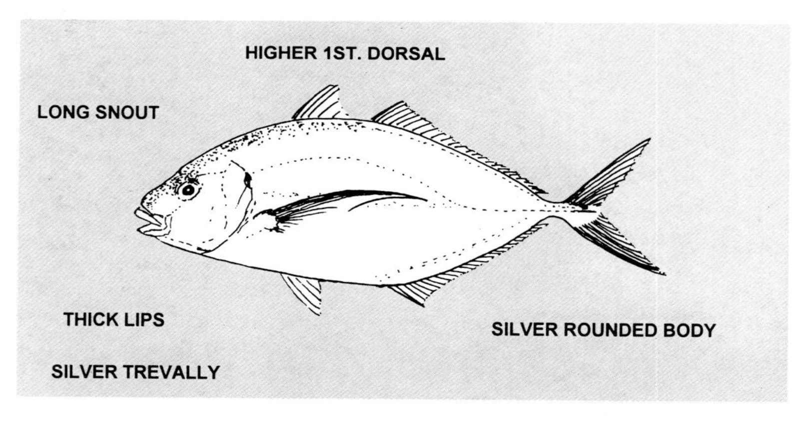

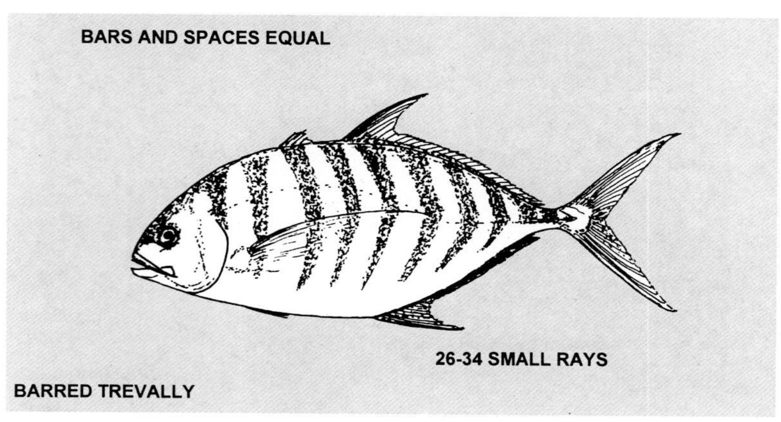

Two other jacks are easy to identify. One is the **golden** trevally (*Gnathadon speciosus*), whose alternating thick and thin vertical stripes against a creamy background is unique to jacks in the Pacific. If you are in doubt, this jack doesn't have any teeth. The second most easily identified trevally is the thicklip or **yellow-spotted** trevally (*Carangoides orthogrammus*), a wide, rounded pompano with distinct lemon-colored spots positioned just after the pectoral fins. My son Derek and my friend Jeff Konn have caught all tackle records for this fish.

The yellow-spotted trevally has thick lips and sometimes is confused with the **silver** trevally (*Psuedocaranx dentex*). But the silver trevally lacks the lemon spots and width of *C. orthogrammus* and it has a distinct black spot at the middle edge of its gill cover.

Another trevally that has the same shape and family as the yellow-spot trevally is the **barred** trevally (*Carangoides ferdau*). It has vertical bands of dark and light which are approximately equal in width. This is a deeper water jack and is only occasionally caught around the reef.

A trevally which is common in the Pacific is the **big-eye** trevally, *C. sexfaciatus*, which, not surprisingly, is an active night feeder. In the Pagoda restaurant in Honolulu, Hawai'i there is a specimen that is over 15 lbs., a world record! The big-eye can be identified by its larger eye, a small, white coloration on the tip of its dorsal fin and a dark spot on the shoulder just behind the gill cover. The flesh of the big-eye trevally is a salmon pink. It is not very good eating.

The **brassy** trevally (*Caranx Papuensis*) is common in the islands south of the equator. This fish is a wonderful fighter on light tackle. It can be distinguished by its yellowish-to-silvery color with small black dots scattered across its upper body. The tail is big for its body and the upper caudal fin is uniformly dark. On the shoulder just behind the gill cover is a pale spot. I caught an alltackle record for the brassy trevally of 7 lbs. 8 oz. off Ovalau in Fiji.

A trevally that is common from Fiji west to Australia is the **gold spot** trevally (*Carangoides fulvoguttatus*) called turrum in Australia. It is sometimes mistaken for the giant trevally because it can weigh over 20 lbs. However, it has many rust-colored spots on its side and the number of dorsal rays is close to 30, while the giant trevally has about 20 dorsal rays.

Two species of **African Pompano** are caught in the Pacific. These are the threadfin or kagami ulua (*Alectis indica* and *Alectis ciliaris*). This is one of the few jacks that is the same in the Pacific as it is in the Atlantic. When this diamond pennant fish is young, it has been described as the most beautiful fish in the world. Long filaments stream from its dorsal and anal fins. Like a kitten that grows into a cat, however, the adult changes dramatically and starts to look and act tough. These two trevallys are difficult to tell apart, but you can check to see how far the eye lies away from the

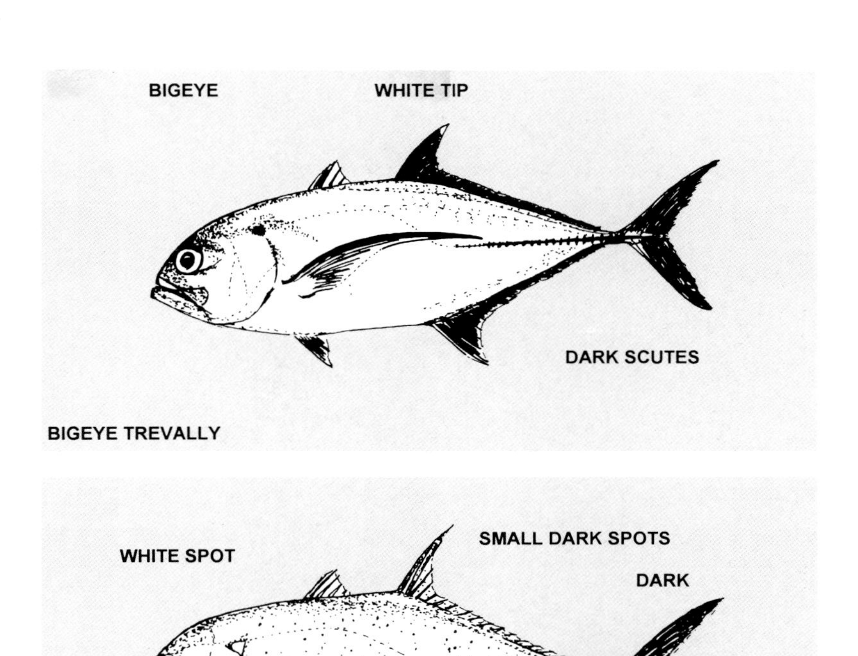

BIGEYE TREVALLY

BRASSY TREVALLY (SAGA)

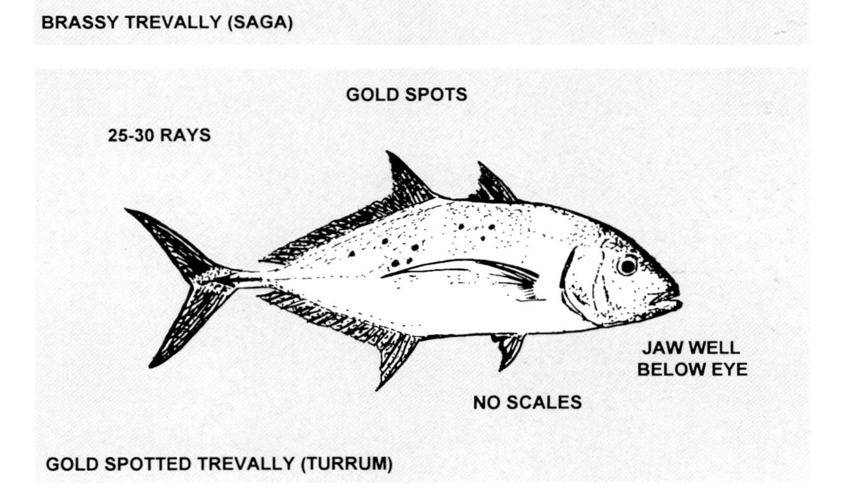

GOLD SPOTTED TREVALLY (TURRUM)

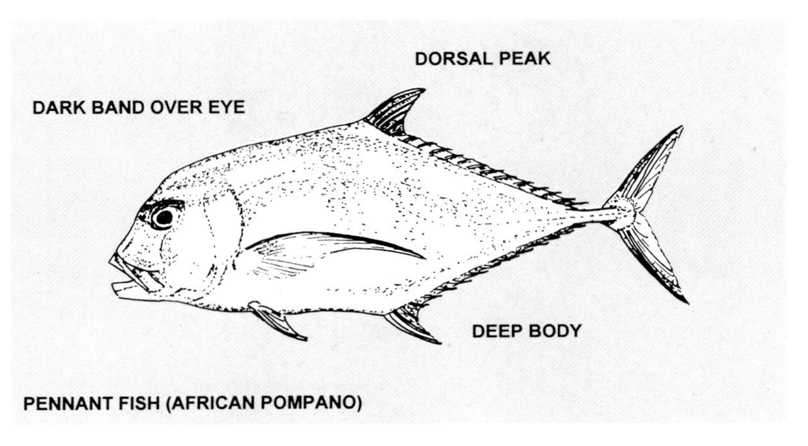

PENNANT FISH (AFRICAN POMPANO)

mouth of the fish. If the eye is within two eye diameters, it is *ciliaris*. *Indica* has a pronounced hump over its eye. *Alectis* is the more common fish and has a dark band above the eye.

All these jacks are good, scrappy gamefish. While there are close to 40 trevally that could be caught in the Pacific, these ten are the largest and most prolific. Of these, the most common are the bluefin, giant, brassy, and bigeye trevally. All of these trevally have been caught with surface lures and for most of them all-tackle world records are waiting for someone to come along and land a big one. I have yet to catch a brassy trevally north of the equator, but they are prolific south from Tonga to New Guinea.

Classification of Family Carangidae

Genus	Species	Local Names
Alectis	ciliaris	African Pompano
Carangoides	ferdau	Barred Trevally
Carangoides	fulvoguttatus	Gold spotted trevally
Carangoides	orthogrammus	Thicklip trevally
Caranx	ignoblis	Giant trevally
Caranx	melampygus	Bluefin trevally
Caranx	papuensis	Brassy trevally
Caranx	sexfaciatus	Bigeye trevally
Gnathanodon	speciosus	Golden trevally
Pseudocaranx	dentex	Silver trevally

The brassy trevally hits a surface plug hard, makes long runs and is a good fighter. Kate Martin caught this 6-lb. fish outside Cagabouli Bay, Naingani Island, Fiji.

Lessons about 'Omilu and Ulua

The two greatest reef predators in the Pacific are the bluefin trevally (*Caranx melampygus*) and the giant trevally (*Caranx ignoblis*). The bluefin can be found all over the Pacific from the Coast of Panama, where it is called the cobalt jack, to the Aldabra reef north of Madagascar near the African Coast. It is found in the Northwest Hawaiian Islands and as far south as Rarotonga. The giant trevally (ulua) is prolific from Hawai'i west to the African Coast.

Both of these fish are prized food fish, grow fast, and are aggressive hunters. In a scientific paper, James Parrish and others related some

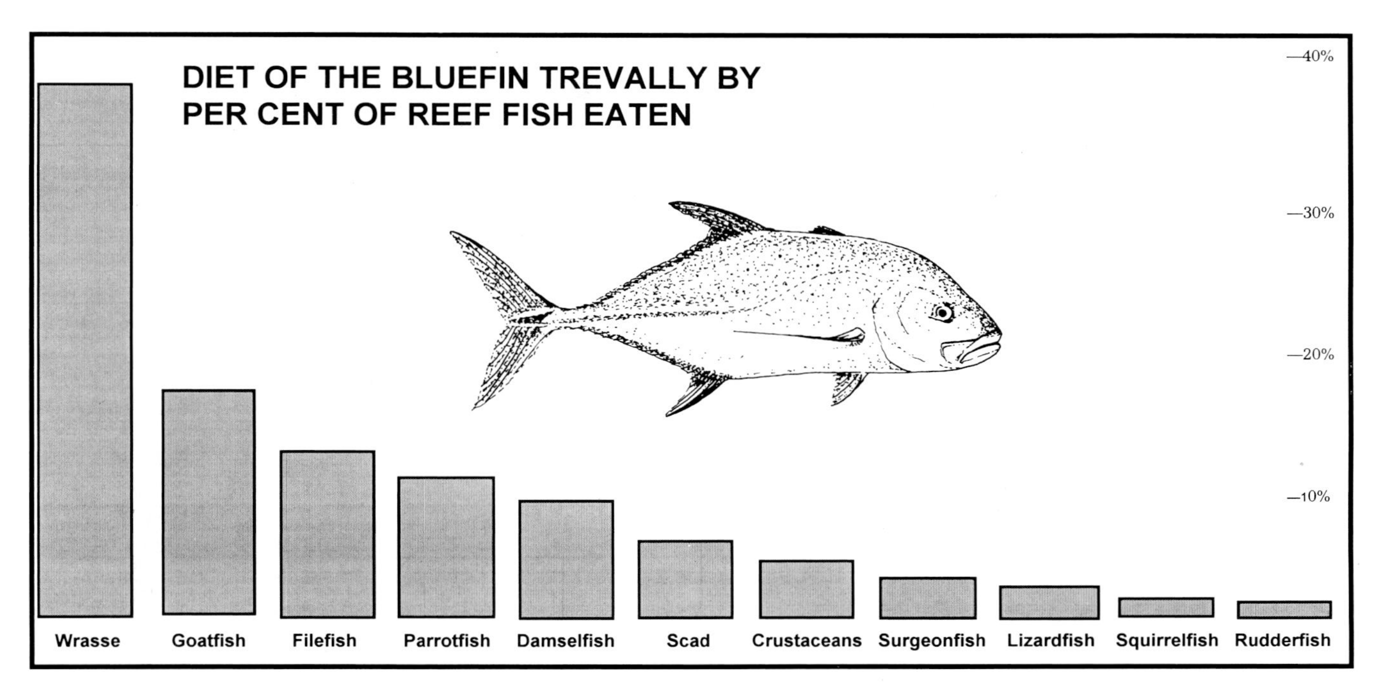

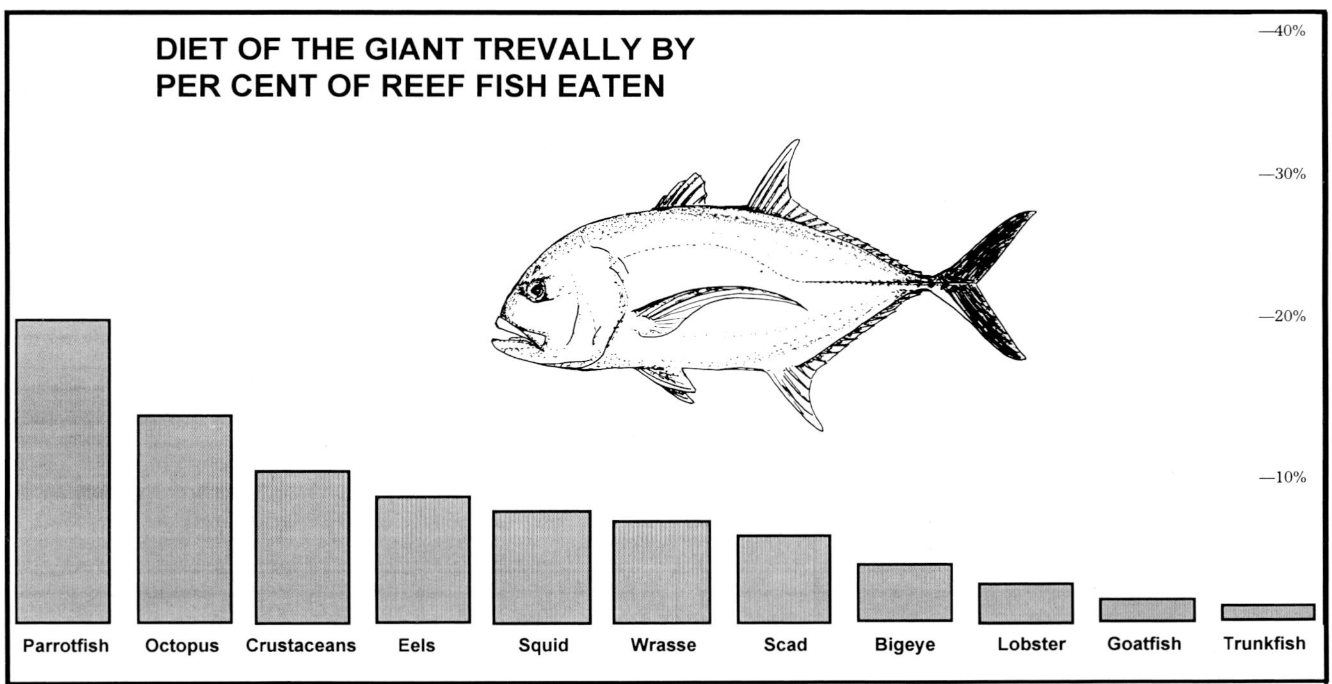

This figure compares the diets of the two most common reef predators.

interesting details about these famous jacks (Fishery Bulletin, 89(3), 1991). Most important is the finding that 90 percent of the diet of both fish are other smaller fish. Through a census of fish on French Frigate Shoals in the Northwest Hawaiian Islands, the authors estimate there are 230,000 bluefin trevally and 130,000 giant trevally on this small reef (about 25 miles in diameter). By carefully examining the stomach contents of a large sample of fish, they further estimate that on French Frigate Shoals these two species eat about 185,000 lbs. of fish per day, or over 30,000 metric tons each year!

But what fish do these jacks eat? The figures show the percent of reef fish that constitute the diet of both predators. The graphs show that wrasse and parrotfish are the most commonly eaten prey of both trevallys. This made me realize that my lures should be much more colorful since these two prey fishes are often brilliantly colored. The predators also eat goatfish and bigeyed scad and squirrelfish. It is therefore advisable to include some lures with big eyes.

There is some overlap in the diets of the large jacks, but the two main species are usually found in different locations. The bluefin never eats any deep-water prey. His diet is almost exclusively reef fish. When the blue jack is young, its diet may also include a few shrimp.

The giant trevally, on the other hand, likes to feed on octopus, eels, and squid. The big predator also eats crabs and lobsters. Lures that can emulate a squid or eel should do very well on the reef.

The group of researchers also measured the age, weight and length of the trevally and determined when they were old enough to spawn. Just how big can a giant trevally get? Based on the authors' predictions, a giant trevally could get as large as 260 pounds! The largest bluefin trevally is estimated to be 38 pounds. So we can pretty well tell that world records are still out there waiting to be caught.

The age of captured fish was determined by counting the rings in the earbones (otolith). Age was then related to the length and weight of the fish. For the first two years both fish grow at almost the same rate. At the end of two years both trevallys weigh a little over two pounds and are a little over a foot long. After three years, the growth rate of the bluefin tapers off, while the giant trevally keeps growing.

Our guide, Mark W. Baxter of Aitutaki, holds his 14-lb. 'omilu

A 22-lb. bluefin trevally, for example, is approximately 7½ yrs. old, about 30 in. long and eats about 13 oz. of fish per day. A giant trevally, on the other hand, at age 7½ yrs. weighs 55 lbs. and eats an average of 1.4 lbs. of prey per day.

Both species of fish spawn during the summer (May, June, and July in the northern hemisphere). Like most fish, the larger they are, the greater the percentage of eggs they produce. These findings suggest that fishermen not be allowed to net gravid fish during the summer and that we return larger fish, which are heavy with roe, back to the sea. Conversely, smaller fish are not yet able to spawn and are excellent eating.

I believe these findings are quite accurate. I know that in recent years heavy commercial and recreational fishing for large trevallys has occurred

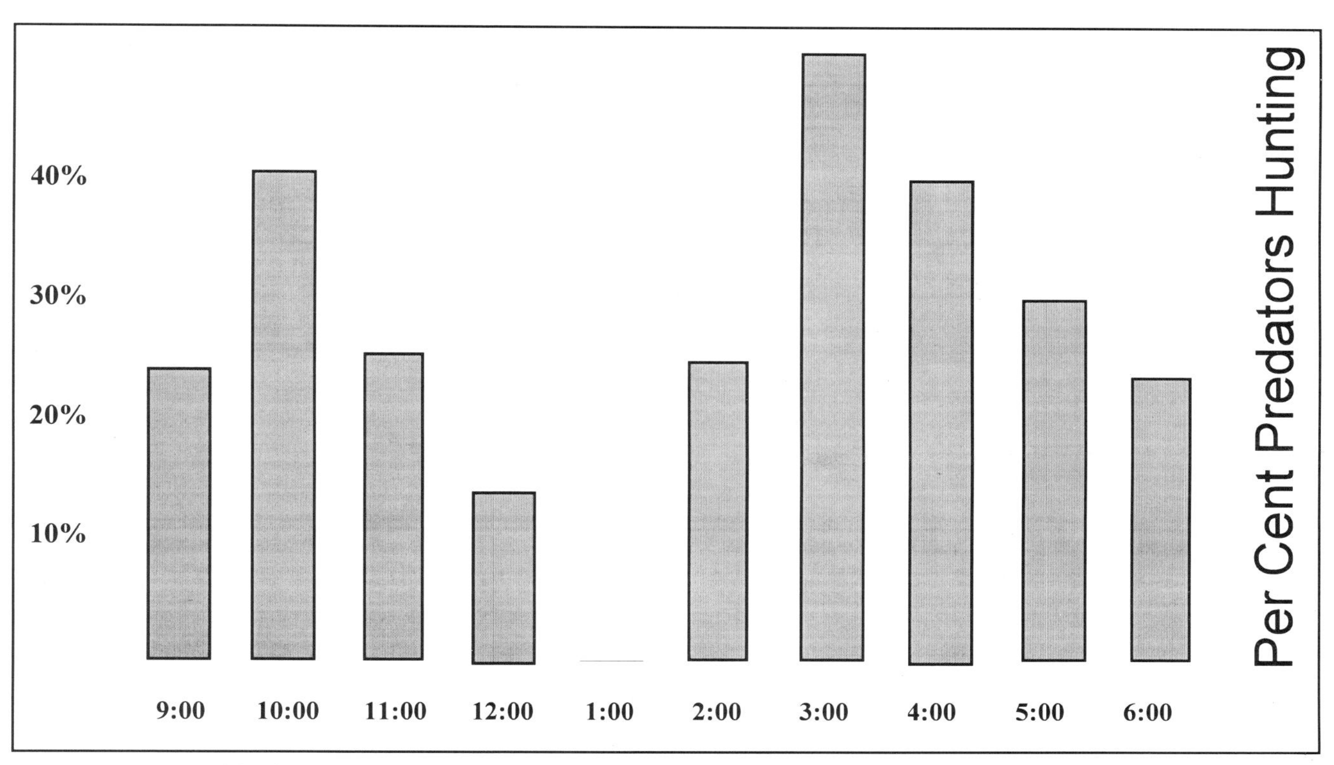

This chart shows that lunch time 12:30 to 1:30 p.m. is not a good time to go fishing. Little is known, however, about the hours before sunset and after sunrise. I have also caught these predators at night using topwater lures.

close to the port of London on Christmas Island in Kiribati. When I went there recently it was difficult to catch the giant trevally.

At the same time, there appeared to be an explosion of smaller reef fish and the light tackle spinning was spectacular. The smaller fish that these predators feed on seemed to be everywhere, as goatfish, snappers, wrasse, and small papio hit our lures at random.

What can we learn from these studies? (1) If you want to catch either of these two trevallys, match the bait to the type and size of fish. A colorful large lure with big eyes seems appropriate. (2) Fish on or close to the reef for the bluefin('omilu). The giant trevally may, however, be in deeper water fronting the reef. (3) When large, mature fish gather in schools during the spring and summer months, they should be allowed to spawn and netting should be prohibited. (4) Unless a giant trevally is a trophy fish, it should be released back into the sea so that it can continue to produce. It is better to take smaller, immature papio for eating. They taste better and are also less likely to contain the ciguatera toxin. (5) Because smaller reef fish constitute the major part of the predator's diet, the general conservation of all kinds of reef fishes is in order so that these fighters can continue to flourish.

Hunting Behavior of Blue Jacks

Aldabra is a remote reef in the Indian Ocean off the east coast of Africa. Both the white ulua (giant trevally) and the 'omilu (bluefin trevally) are plentiful on the Aldabra reef. Over a three-month period, G. W. Potts, a zoologist, dove on the reef using SCUBA gear and wrote about the hunting behavior of the bluefin trevally (Potts, 1979, 1980, 1981).

Some of the results of his observations are fascinating. For example, of the hundreds of trevally Potts observed, none were seen hunting prey from high noon until 1:00 p.m. The following figure shows that the 'omilu's daytime hunting behavior had two peaks, one at 10:30 a.m. and one at about 2:00 p.m., but dropped dramatically at midday. We don't know much about the fish's behavior in the early morning or evening, but I suspect these are also good times to fish. I have caught both the blue jack and the giant trevally at night, as well.

Potts also found a direct relationship between the size of the fish eaten and the size of the predator fish. The larger the trevally, the larger the bait fish that was pursued.

Potts indicated that *Caranx* like to hunt downstream or up-current but not crosscurrent. He related that the predators rarely made more than two attacks. Bluefin (*Caranx melampygus*) swim slowly and stalk their prey to get as close as possible before charging. Often the bluefin will use the shadow of a rock as a hiding place from which to ambush prey fish. Once the small reef fish panics, a Caranx will accelerate rapidly. This is called the "attacking chain." As the prey fish swims faster, so does *Caranx*.

Potts also observed that the large jacks are "piscivorous" or almost exclusively fish eaters. Most prey fish are taken in one gulp. The 'omilu and ulua are active in dim light which occurs in early morning and evenings. They are also more active just after low tide.

Potts summarized the visual characteristic that attract 'omilu:

- a small, moving fish shape
- a bait that is isolated
- sudden movements
- easily seen relative to background

What does all this mean to the fisherman? Fishermen should use an active, jerky lure that resembles available bait fish. The lure can be moved slowly at first but should rapidly accelerate thereafter. Casts should be made to the edges of dominant shadowy rocks and outcroppings where the jacks may be hiding. Casts should be made down the swell of the wave that breaks on the reef' but not across it. Casts should be made from a long way away so that the bait seems isolated.

Because ulua and 'omilu have a feeding circuit that they patrol, the fisherman should come back to likely spots, areas that have had fish in them before.

Another important point is the fact that the larger trevally were found to prey on larger bait

Derek Dunn-Rankin catches a 7-lb. bluefin trevally off Naigani Island, Fiji. Note the light-blue color that this fish displays.

fish. Small prey, around 2 or 3 in. long, were unafraid of the larger bluefins. This means that a lure that is larger than most fishermen use (4 to 8 in. long) should be used to catch the big jacks.

Finally, it seems reasonable to conclude that when the sun is high in the sky, it is time to get under some shade, eat some lunch and maybe take a nap.

Barracuda

The great barracuda (*Sphyraena barracuda*) reaches lengths of seven feet and weighs over 80 lbs. This slashing fighter inhabits all the reefs of the Pacific, and is another worldwide gamefish. It can be found lying in the deeper water of the passes, or along the reef's edge waiting for prey. The "cuda's" initial runs are long and fast. Their teeth can make mincemeat of most nylon leaders, and I have found the fish difficult to bring

The blackfin barracuda is prolific below the equator. This fish can weigh more than 25 lbs.

The great barracuda can cut through a monofilament leader like a hot knife through butter.

to gaff. In the passes of Pohnpei big barracuda seemed everywhere. Three times in one afternoon I had fish slice right through 80-lb. mono leader just in front of the lure and then leave the lure floating on the surface. We retrieved the lure but lost the fish. A short (18 in.) steel or cable leader may be necessary to land the big one.

The great barracuda is distinguished from its closest relative, the chevron barracuda or blackfin barracuda (*Sphyraena putnamiae*), by the black splotches on its body and its truncated caudal fin, that is, the tailfin is not indented. If you are still in doubt, the chevron cuda's dog teeth slant backwards whereas the great barracuda's fangs are straight. The chevron barracuda has about 20 chevron-shaped bars on the upper two-thirds of its silvery body. Its caudal fin is indented and has a black margin. This fish can reach five feet in length

Sharks

I know three reef sharks that will pursue a surface lure. They are the **black tip reef** shark (*Carcharhinus melanopterus*), **the gray reef** shark (*Carcharhinus amblyrhnchos*) and the **silver tip** shark (*Carcharhinus albimarginatus*). Each of these sharks will aggressively pursue a big lure over a short run, making waves eddy out behind them. If you don't jerk the lure out of their mouths and you use a big lure so that their teeth cannot find the leader, you can land quite a big fish on relatively light gear.

The **black tip reef shark** is the most easily identified because the tips of its dorsal, pectoral and caudal fins are edged in a dark brown. The silver tip is another whaler shark but its high dorsal fin, pectoral fins and caudal fins are tipped in white. It differs from the white tip reef shark because the whitetip does not show white on its pectoral fins and because the white tip is a slender, bottom-dwelling shark with a large second dorsal fin.

Richard Murakami shows the blacktip reef shark he caught off Peleliu in Belau.

The **gray reef** shark is a grayish-brown shading to white. Its dorsal fin has a unique shape. It is rounded in front but the back drops sharply, making an acute angle. The trailing edge of the caudal fin has a broad black margin. These sharks are found all over the Pacific but are more prevalent in certain areas. Pohnpei and Belau have their share of sharks, but I also saw a few in Fiji. Sharks are just now being recognized as gamefish, and these agile animals will attack surface lures that are large enough to see clearly.

One of the best ways to attract a reef shark is to throw a lure up into shallow water and drag it slowly off the reef into the break and beyond. You almost always see the shark go for the lure and you can decide whether or not to try and land them. If you retrieve the lure at top speed they will not pursue for any distance.

The Pacific Houndfish or Needlefish

Some species of the small needlefish we see on the surface of the bays and warm estuaries can grow to over 4 ft. in length. The Pacific houndfish or crocodile long-tom (*Tylosurus crocodilus*) is among the most acrobatic fighters in the sea. Inshore, the fish has a green coloration, but off the reef, outside, it acquires a deep purple blue and silver color. Surprisingly, the needlefish are delicious eating. Their long jaws make them difficult to hook but the fish are very aggressive and, when nothing else strikes within the warm thermocline of the surface, the long tom will still be hitting.

Twice I have caught the keel jawed needlefish (*tylosaurus melanotus*) which has a distinct flat bony keel on the tip of its lower jaw.

The houndfish can weigh as much as 14 lbs.

Groupers

More groupers (known as rock cod) are lost in the coral reef than any other fish because they like to duck into a hole in the coral and then the line gets cut or broken trying to get them out. The **peacock grouper** (*Cephalopholis argus*), sometimes called the peacock rockcod, is a purplish black fish covered with small, bright-blue spots. It is common throughout the Pacific and can be caught in fairly shallow water. These fish reach about 5 lbs. They are aggressive, and my friend,

George Mendreshora caught two peacock groupers on one lure. He was fishing the inside reef south of Cook Island, Christmas Atoll, Kiribati.

George Mendrehsora, once caught two of these fish on one surface lure!

The **coral trout** (*Plectropomus leopardus*) can be distinguished from the **peacock cod** by its lighter color and truncated tail. The tail (caudal fin) of the **coral trout** is vertically straight. **Coral trout** are terrific fighters and very few fish over ten pounds are caught on spinning gear when using long poles because the "give" in the pole and stretch in the line allows them to dash for cover in the coral. These fish are good eating. The meat is soft and white and needs to be iced quickly.

I have caught many **banded groupers** spinning over the reef. There are as many as 30 species in the family *Epineheus*. Specific identification is difficult without a good reference.

Derek had to swim out and untangle this 8-lb. coral trout from around the coral heads.

I use four primary references: (1) Tinker, S. W., 1972; (2) Grant, E. M., 1987; (3) Randall, J. E., et al., 1990 and (4) Matsuda, H, et al., 1984 (see References inside the back cover).

All sorts of banded groupers are available on the reef.

The **bluetailed cod** (*E. microdon*) and the **banded grouper** (*E. moara*) have been caught several times on surface lures off Belau and Fiji.

The **coronation trout** (*Variola louti*) looks a lot like the coral trout but its caudal fin is curved and the margin or edge is bright yellow-orange. I

The largest coronation trout on record. It weighed 21-lbs.

This 18-lb. snapper hit a LOLO lure on the surface in 35 ft. of water.

have caught this fish spinning, but the largest fish on record, 21 lbs., was caught drifting a small bonefish as bait off the Cook Island Reef at Christmas Island.

Snappers

Snappers can be found in and along the edges of the coral reef. The giant **red snapper** (*Lutjanus bohar*) will come to the surface in water over 40 feet deep to grab a surface lure. The trick then is to keep this enterprising predator from reaching the bottom again. Any slack in the line is quickly taken advantage of by *Lutjanidae*. Snappers easily reach weights over 15-lbs. This red bass has been justifiably implicated in ciguatera fish poisoning. I tested these fish in Palmyra and the red snappers there had the highest readings.

The **Maori seaperch** (*L. rivulatus*) has been caught on shallow inner reefs of Fiji and gives a great fight. The fish can be distinguished by the pattern of bright-blue wavy lines that cross the face like a Maori tattoo. The red bass or snapper (*L. bohar*) is recognized by the conspicuous deep pit just before each eye and its fiery rose-red color.

The Maori seaperch is a shallow water reef fighter. This one was caught off Horseshoe Reef, Fiji.

Emperors

The **Emperors** (*Lethrinus*) or "sweet lips" are shallow reef dwellers and good fighters. They can be taken in the backwash of breaking waves on incoming tide and they are a prized food fish. The orange red-mouthed **yellowlip emperor** is the most common on the reef (*L. xanthochilus*). All members of the family *Lethrinus* can be identified by scaleless cheeks and protruding snout. The **long nose emperor** (*L. olivaceus*) is a dull greenish color with a slender body and unusually long snout. Jeff Konn caught a 10-lb. 11-oz. long nose near the Korean Wreck at the bottom of Christmas Island

This yellowlip emperor was an all tackle record. It was caught off Lifuka, Ha'apai, Kingdom of Tonga

that is an all-tackle record and Richard Murakami caught an 8-lb. 8-oz. all-tackle yellow "sweet lips" off the horseshoe reef in Fiji. On a trip to Tonga I hauled in a 12-lb. yellowlip on the leeward reef off the Lifuka Island causeway.

Pelagic Fish

The free-swimming ocean fishes sometimes congregate near the reefs of the Pacific as they search for food. Tunas, wahoo, and rainbow runners have been caught casting near or from coral reefs. Sometimes schools of tuna can be found

Skipjack tuna can also be found hitting surface lures.

inside the larger lagoons. If you are in a boat and you see the water boiling as yellowfin tuna (ahi) attack schools of baitfish, then stop and cast into this action for good results. I have caught big yellowfin casting inside the lagoon at Pohnpei and Palau and just outside the reefs of many atolls.

The key to catching these blue torpedoes is to get within casting distance, stop the motor, and drift. The sound of the boat drives the fish down. Staying just outside the melee and tossing a lure 70 to 80 yds. allows anglers to catch several fish. Unfortunately, sharks patrol under the slashing attacks of the tuna and my record is that I lose about a third of the fish hooked to sharks. The yellowfin or Allison tuna has a very long pectoral fin and yellow margins to its curved dorsal and anal fins.

Other tunas, the **skipjack** (*Katsuwonus pelamis*), **mackerel** tuna (*Euthynnus affinis*), and

dogtooth tuna (*gyimnosarda unicolor*) also have been caught close to the reef. The skipjack tuna is known immediately by the four or more long stripes on its belly. The dogtooth tuna is known for its large doglike conical teeth. Mackerel tuna are

Yellowfin or Allison tuna can be caught next to the reef when they attack schools of bait fish.

immediately identified by a large oval patch on the back above the lateral line that contains a series of dark, wavy broken lines.

Wahoo and Barred Mackerel

Wahoo (*Acanthocybium solandri*) have been caught off the edges of reefs all over the Pacific but they are more often caught trolling while moving from one place to another than they are by spinning to the edge of the reef.

Taniquique is the Pacific's equivalent of the Atlantic's king mackerel. This narrow-barred Spanish mackerel (*Scomberomorus commerson*) frequents the South Pacific reefs and is often caught in and around the deeper edges of the coral. Taniquique can reach sizes over 100 lbs. and are sometimes mistaken for **wahoo**. It has, however, a much shorter snout and only 15 to 18 dorsal spines.

The Pacific Spanish mackerel is a distant cousin to the Atlantic king fish.

It is more deep bodied and has numerous thin, wavy bars across its body. These fish are caught in the 30-lb. range all year around off Fiji's sunken reefs.

Rainbow Runners

I have caught rainbow runners right off the reef at Christmas Island. These spectacular fighting fish stay on the surface and therefore a large fish can be landed. Rainbow runners are distinguished by two narrow, light-blue stripes along the sides with a yellowish stripe in between. They have a large forked tail and no scutes or central ridges at the base of the tail.

Leatherskin or Queenfish

The leatherskin or lai (Hawai'i) is a swift darting fish that will hit almost any small lure. The double-spotted queenfish (*Scomberoides lysan*) has dusky round blotches on its silvery sides both above and below its lateral line. It can separated from the giant queenfish (*Scomeroides commersonianus*) because the upper half of its dorsal fin is darkly pigmented. These fish make for great light tackle action and can attain weights over 10 lbs.

Other Game Fish

Wrasse

Wrasse (*Labridae*) are abundant. Except for gobies, there are more species of wrasse than other fish on the reef. Only a few of the wrasses, however, prey on other fish. Chief among these is the **maori** wrasse (*Cheilinus undulatus*). These fish can grow to weigh over 300 lbs.When wrasse are younger, they are fairly aggressive and will attack surface lures. They are usually olive green, with a large rounded caudal fin. The head is blue to blue-green, with irregular yellowish lines all across its face. A large, protruding hump on the forehead is seen in adults. I caught one of these wrasse, an 8 lb. fish, off Kepara Island in Pohnpei. We put it on the grill, skin and all, and when it had steamed, we peeled off the charcoaled covering and ate the white meat inside with chopsticks. It was delicious.

Bonefish

While bonefish (*Albula*) will rarely attack surface lures, they will hit jigs and touts in the shallow water of the lagoons of the line island chain, and on the inner lagoons in Hawai'i. Since you can spin for these silver streaks and see all the action, they qualify for inclusion. Several times I have caught bonefish over 8 lbs. by using the tail of the hermit crab for bait. Use a small hook and stalk the bonefish. When you see the fish tailing make a soft cast and you may be off to the races.

Bonefish can be caught on the sand flats

A WORLD RECORD FOR ANY ANGLER

World records used to be so elusive that only the very rich or the very lucky could get one. That was because the IGFA recognized only a very few fish as true gamefish. These were the spectacular billfish (sailfish and marlin) and the big bluefin tunas out of Bimini and some shoreline fish such as stripers, barracuda, and tarpon.

In 1983, only 153 fresh and saltwater all-tackle world records were maintained by the International Gamefish Association. That has changed. In the latest IGFA's Yearbook, *World Record Gamefish*, over 500 all-tackle world records are presented and the number is growing.

There are two kinds of world records, **line-class** records and **all-tackle** records. Where almost any commonly caught fighting fish can qualify for an all-tackle record, there are less than 100 different fish that have been admitted to line-class status. It is really tough to set or break a line-class record. I know, because I tried for five years before I caught an 'omilu (blue finned trevally) big enough to qualify. With line-class record fish, the angler is limited to certain line strengths (2-,4-,6-,8-,16-,20- and 30-lb. test line, for example).

All-tackle records, however, allow the angler to use any line up to 130-lb. test and is open to any trophy fish that are commonly caught on rod and reel (handlining is not allowed). This lets the public decide what is a good fighting fish, and all this knowledge is important scientifically. The only restriction is that the fish should be a big one, a trophy fish. The IGFA defines that as being in the upper half of the maximum weight attained by a particular species of fish.

Let's take an example. Nuenue (**Pacific Chub**) is a terrific fighter and is commonly fished for in Hawai'i. You are out fishing and you land a big one, say 9 lbs. This could be an all-tackle world record. I don't know how big nuenue can grow but I have seen some in Hanauma Bay, O'ahu, that would be close to 10 lbs. So I believe a nine pounder would qualify.

Half the trouble of getting a world record is in the application. You need to weigh and measure the fish in front of witnesses, take a picture of the fish, fill out the application and have it notarized. This takes time and you need to make sure that the scale you use has been tested by the scale company or certified by the state.

I have a couple of Chatillion spring scales that I purchased from the Young Scale company in Kaimuki, O'ahu. Before fishing in areas where there may not be a certified scale, I have the scale company check my scales to see if they are measuring accurately. But almost all grocery stores have certified scales and are usually happy to weigh a potential world record. Restaurants are another good source for certified scales. I am told that the fish auction in downtown Honolulu is open 24 hrs. a day and it has a certified scale.

In 1982, my son Derek caught a yellowspot trevally inside the reef on the North shore of Christmas Island. This papio weighed almost six pounds and we submitted it to the IGFA as an entry in their annual fishing contest. Since this was a new species, it qualified for an all-tackle record. Jim House, mate of the *No-Ka-Oi-IV*, told me that he caught the same species off Maui that might have been close to 10 lbs. So Derek's record was made to be broken. Richard Murakami caught a big sweet lips on our last trip to Fiji and this 7½-pounder became an all-tackle world record.

IGFA World Record & Fishing Contest Application

FORM FOR RECORDING FRESHWATER & SALTWATER GAME FISH CATCHES

Read all IGFA angling rules and world record requirements before completing and signing this application. The angler's signature on the completed form must be witnessed by a notary. This application must be accompanied by line or tippet samples and photographs as specified in the World Record Requirements. Hybrids and other species which may pose a problem of identity should be examined by an ichthyologist or qualified fishery biologist.

I AM SUBMITTING THIS ENTRY FOR:

☐ An all-tackle world record.

☐ A world record in the following line class:

__________ lb/ __________ kg

☐ A fly rod world record in the following tippet class:

__________ lb/ __________ kg

☐ Annual Contest ☐ Catch & Release

☐ 5-1 Club ☐ 10-1 Club ☐ 15-1 Club ☐ 20-1 Club

☐ 10 Pound Bass Club ☐ Thousand Pound Club

SPECIES

Common name: __________

Scientific name: __________

WEIGHT: Fish was weighed in ☐ lbs ☐ kgs.

lbs: __________ oz: __________ kg: __________

Digital weight (if weighed on electronic scales, give weight exactly as shown): __________

DATE OF CATCH: __________

PLACE OF CATCH: __________

____

LENGTH (See measurement diagrams)

inches: x to x __________ xx to xx __________

cm: x to x __________ xx to xx __________

GIRTH (See measurement diagrams)

inches: __________ cm: __________

METHOD OF CATCH (trolling, casting, fly fishing, etc.): __________

FIGHTING TIME: __________

ANGLER (Print name as you wish it to appear on your record or contest certificate:

____

Permanent address
(Include country and address code):

____

____

____

Angler's fishing club affiliation (if any):

____

EQUIPMENT

Rod

Make: __________

Tip length (center of reel to end of tip): __________

Butt length (center of reel to lower end of butt):

____

Reel

Make: __________ Size: __________

Line or tippet

Make: __________ Size as stated on label: __________

☐ I am an IGFA member, enclosed is $10

☐ I am not an IGFA member, enclosed is $25

Enclosed is $_______ check or money order for the World Record application processing fee.

or

Please charge to my __Visa __Mastercard __American Express

Account No. ☐☐☐☐☐☐☐☐☐☐☐☐☐☐☐☐

Expiration date_________Signature__________

Note: All items must be filled in. If an item does not apply, write "none used". Do not leave any spaces blank.

Length of double line: ______________

Make of backing: ______________ Size: ______

Other equipment:

Type of gaff: ______________ Length: ______

Length of trace or leader: ______________

Number and type of hooks: ______________

Name of lure, fly or bait: ______________

BOAT (if used)

Name: ______________

Make: ______________ Length: ______

Captain's name: ______________

Signature: ______________

Address: ______________

____

Mate's name: ______________

Signature: ______________

Address: ______________

____

SCALES

Location: ______________

Type: ______________

Manufacturer: ______________

Date last certified: ______________

Person and/or agency that certified scales:

____

Weighmaster: ______________

Signature: ______________

Address: ______________

____

WITNESSES

Witness to weighing (other than angler, captain or weighmaster): ______________

Address: ______________

____

Witnesses to catch (other than captain). List two names and addresses if possible.

1. ______________

____

2. ______________

____

Number of persons witnessing catch: ______

VERIFICATION OF SPECIES IDENTITY
(See world record requirements.)

Signature of examining ichthyologist:

____

Title, degree, or qualifications: ______________

Address: ______________

____

AFFIDAVIT

I, the undersigned, hereby take oath and attest that the fish described in this application was hooked, fought, and brought to gaff by me without assistance from anyone, except as specifically provided in the regulations; and that it was caught in accordance with IGFA angling rules; and that the line submitted with this application is the actual line used to catch the fish on the stated date. I further declare that all the information in this application is true and correct to the best of my knowledge. I understand that IGFA reserves the right to employ verification procedures. I agree to be bound by any ruling of the IGFA relative to this application.

Signature of angler: ______________

Sworn before me this ______________ day of ______________ 19______.

Notary signature and seal: ______________

When completely filled out and signed, mail this application with photos and line sample by quickest means to:
INTERNATIONAL GAME FISH ASSOCIATION, 1301 East Atlantic Blvd., Pompano Beach, Florida 33060 USA

(This application may be reproduced.)

When I was in Fiji I caught two fish that everyone said were trophy size. One was an 11½-lb. blackfin barracuda. This fish doesn't grow as large as the giant barracuda and it differs from its more familiar cousin since its tail is forked and its body is banded with chevrons. The other trophy was an almost 7-lb. long tom, a 4-ft. long needle fish (*crocodilus*). These two fish became the initial all-tackle world records that have since been surpassed. Someone in Hawai'i caught a needlefish over 14 lbs.!

Knowing the maximum size for a given fish is important to the scientific community. Zoology professor Jim Parrish at the University of Hawai'i is interested in the size of giant trevallys and can now predict their age by knowing their length and weight. This tells us how fast such fish grow and lends insight into how their population may need to be managed in order to maintain the survival of the species. The 'omilu, for example, is said to obtain weights of 30 lbs. in the Northwest Hawaiian Islands. And an old-timer told me he saw a picture of one that weighed 42 lbs.! For other fish, little is known about just how big they can get.

Accurate data, however, are needed to establish weight claims and all-tackle records are one such means. There are a number of fish that are commonly caught in and around Hawai'i and the South Pacific that should qualify for all-tackle world records. You can xerox a copy of the IGFA's application form from any of their recent yearbooks or use the one provided in this text. Note that there is an application processing fee for both members and non-members of the IGFA. You may also qualify for the yearly tournament. Awards are given for the three largest fish.

In filling out a world record application, remember to :

- weigh and measure the fish in front of witnesses on a certified scale;
- take a picture of the fish;
- fill out the application and have it notarized;
- send application, picture and some of the line you used to the IGFA.

This takes time but it is worth it.

All-tackle entries also help establish line class fish. If the IGFA gets a great many applications for all-tackle world records for a particular species, they think seriously about establishing distinct line class records for these fish. It was at the urging of Pacific anglers that the bluefin trevally was established as a line class fish. Now, records are recorded for this fish in line classes from 2- to 30-lb. test. For information on line class and all-tackle records, consult the

Ron Lum holds on to a big 'omilu spinning off the western reef of Aitutaki, Cooks.

A 30-lb. trevally caught near the ruins of Nan-Madol in Pohnpei, Micronesia.

IGFA's latest yearbook. The next time you go spinning, be prepared to submit an application for an all-tackle record.

Catch and Release

When I was a young boy living in Surfside, Miami Beach, mullet by the millions poured through the Baker's Haulover, cut and ran north and south as far as the eye could see. We would stand in waist-high water on the sand bars and have the mullet run into us during their annual migrations. Now Tony Stormont, my commercial fishing friend on the East coast, tells me he sees only a small school now and then.

Rudy Gabler's dad used to regularly catch 60-lb. king mackerel from the Haulover bridge, swimming a dead mullet out 200 yds. on the outgoing tide as bait. One day Rudy, now a guide in the Bahamas, nearly swamped his skiff when he handlined 1500 lbs. of kingfish aboard in a couple of hours. Now limits are placed on the fish since the great schools have been decimated.

Old-timers in Hawai'i tell of regularly catching 100 lb. giant trevally off Waimanalo, on O'ahu, record-sized bonefish off Waikiki, world record bluefin trevally off the Yokohama Flats near Kaena Pt. and giant threadfin moi off the north shore. Now all that is gone. Conservation measures have not kept pace with the increase in population.

To continue the recreation of sports fishing, big fish must be released so that they can spawn and perpetuate their species. Fishing resources are limited, especially on small atolls. Catching fish doesn't mean you have to kill the fish. Even record or trophy fish can be weighed, measured, photographed and returned to the sea.

While it is particularly hard to release fish in the South Pacific where islanders' livelihood and diet are highly dependent on fish, all sports fishermen must practice **Catch and Release** so that fishing can be enjoyed for generations to come. By releasing big fish, you protect the environment and its resources and teach others to do the same.

AFTERWORD

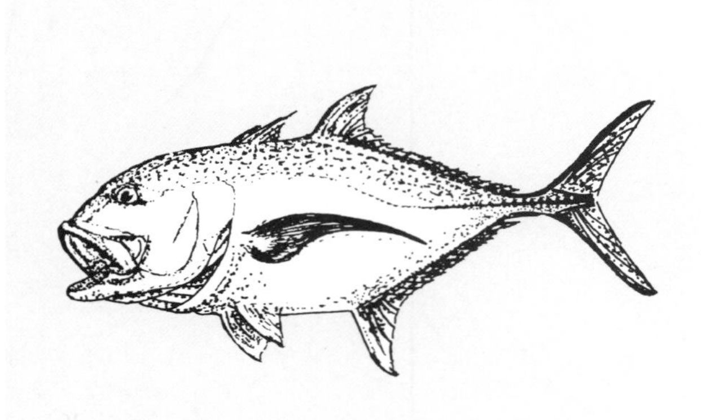

The giant trevally, ulua, is one of the great reef predators. It hits like a tiger and pulls like a bull.

Inventor of the famous Hawaiian **PILI** lure, the resin surface popper which started a revolution in topwater fishing, Peter Dunn-Rankin has traveled the Pacific extensively, learning how and where to catch trophy fish on light gear. Now, in ***Fishing the Reefs,*** he lets everyone in on his fishing secrets.

Six-time IGFA* world-record holder, "Pete" provides specific answers to catching the "bulls" of the reef. He tells the reader how to make and use topwater lures to catch the elusive ulua, 'omilu, great barracuda, black-tip reef shark, grouper, snapper, yellowfin tuna, and Pacific mackerel.

The travel **Checklist** makes this book helpful in planning any fishing adventure. The author's fishing potential rating of the Pacific islands is especially valuable in selecting the angler's dream destination.

The many drawings and photographs make this book enjoyable and informative reading for topwater anglers of all ages. ***Fishing the Reefs*** should be in every fisherman's library.

Jeff Konn

*International Game Fishing Association

Veteran topwater fisherman Jeff Konn and a 16 ½-lb. bluefin trevally caught on 16-lb. test line with a topwater resin lure.